*Praise for*

# PRAYERS DURING A GLOBAL CRISIS
## A 40-Day Prayer Manual to Make It Through Challenging Times

"Prayers During a Global Crisis" is filled with power-packed prayers that really stir one's spirit to pray and intercede. The moment I started reading the first page, I thought, **"This is the type of book you have to read out loud and declare."** I immediately began to declare and speak each prayer and Scripture with authority and power. Every Scripture is a pressing reminder of God's promises. This book was birthed in the midst of a pandemic, and you can affirm that those prayers were spoken from a heart that was desperate to see God move and intervene!

The format of the book is set up in such a way that you can read each prayer as a declaration for that day. Each day has a specific theme that hits home and encourages you not to allow your situation to overtake you. It's a courageous reminder that prayer in the midst of adversity can bring change. The power of life and death are in our tongues, and the words in this prayer book speak life! I highly recommend this prayer book to anyone, whether you are struggling to pray, a seasoned intercessor, or someone who longs to see God's will fulfilled on earth.

*Pastors Jose and Sunshine Miranda*
**Northgate Church**
**Hammond, Indiana**

JoAnn sets the tone with a friendly reminder that in times of trouble or chaos, God is in control of everything that happens in this world, and nothing can happen without His approval. The power of prayer is felt when reading each daily journal. It is undeniable that prayer changes us and how we perceive what is going on in the world around us as we reflect on each daily reading and the Scriptures provided. The author reflects on God's goodness, and her transparency thru the sharing of her testimony brings hope and encouragement.

*Jennifer Michael-Vargas,*
**Account Representative, Ria Trufant Insurance Agency**
**Children's Ministry, Northgate Church Hammond, Indiana**
**Jesse Vargas, Journeyman/Mechanic**
**Warfield Electric Company,**
**Hobart, Indiana**

Desperate times call for desperate measures…and in times like this, we need people of prayer who will get on the wall, stay on the wall, and not come down until breakthrough is realized! As the founder and leader of a daily prayer ministry that has been in existence for over twenty years, I know firsthand the time, commitment, energy, boldness, and warfare one must go through as an intercessor and prayer leader. JoAnn has done an incredible job of providing the Body of Christ with a guide to help us pray through times of crisis and come out as overcomers.

*Pastor Kisia L. Coleman,*
**Pray on Warrior, Warrior of Wisdom (P.O.W., W.O.W.)**
**Prayer Ministry Founder,**
**Kingdom Church Int'l. Ministries, Co-Founder,**
**Empowered People Church, Lead Pastor,**
**Richton Park, IL**

JoAnn's words, penned in the midst of a global crisis, remind us that no matter the circumstances, our God is near. He hears our cries, even when our hearts can't find the words. Whether prayer is as familiar to you as your favorite blanket or as new as the morning dew, let JoAnn's powerful, poignant prayers wash over you and renew your spirit, reminding you that you are His child…and He loves you more than you could ever imagine.

*Cynthia Maloy*
**Embracing Abilities, Inc.**
**Avon, Indiana**

## A Special Word from *Bryant and Mandy Figures*
### …JoAnn's loving and devoted parents.

My wife and I truly believe that JoAnn's testimony is one of the most inspirational and spirit-filled words that someone can share to let others know and hear how powerful the Living God is. This book may be one of the most helpful tools you can use in bringing yourself or someone you know closer to a relationship with Jesus Christ. There are many things in life that keep us from pursuing our relationship with God. In this inspiring message and through the highlighted Scriptures of the Bible, you will find out why so many people have chosen to allow God to turn their life around and begun to walk with Jesus. This is the life story of someone who has experienced a season of darkness and decided to let Jesus use her. And even though the enemy attacks from behind, God had her back, as we see in JoAnn today. This book is fascinating. Praise the Lord!

# PRAYERS DURING A GLOBAL CRISIS

*A 40-Day Prayer Manual to Make It Through Challenging Times*

*JoAnn LaTasha Smith-Figures*

*Prayers During a Global Crisis:*
*A 40-Day Prayer Manual to Make It Through Challenging Times*
by JoAnn LaTasha Smith-Figures

Cover design, editing, book layout, and publishing services by KishKnows, Inc., Richton Park, Illinois, 708-252-DOIT

admin@kishknows.com, www.kishknows.com

ISBN 978-0-578-95843-9
LCCN 2021915246

All rights reserved. No part of this book may be reproduced, distributed, or transmitted in any form or by any means, including photocopying, recording, digital scanning, or other electronic or mechanical methods, without the prior written permission of the publisher, except in the case of brief quotations embodied in critical reviews and certain other noncommercial uses permitted by copyright law. For permission requests, please contact JoAnn LaTasha Smith-Figures at *smithjoann344@yahoo.com*.

Some Scripture references may be paraphrased versions or illustrative references of the author. Unless otherwise specified, all other references are from the King James Version of the Bible.

Scriptures marked **NIV** are taken from **THE HOLY BIBLE, NEW INTERNATIONAL VERSION®, NIV®** Copyright© 1973, 1978, 1984, 2011 by Biblica, Inc.® Used by permission. All rights reserved worldwide.

Copyright© 2021 by JoAnn LaTasha Smith-Figures
Printed in the United States of America

# CONTENTS

| | |
|---|---:|
| My Testimony | 1 |
| Dedication | 5 |
| Devotional Readings | 7-167 |
| Resources | 168 |
| About the Author | 169 |
| Contact the Author | 169 |

# MY TESTIMONY

*This devotional* would not have been possible without the divine plan of God. Through Jesus, God has brought me out of the slavery of sin and into the freedom of a relationship with Him. But my story does not end here…my transformation is not over yet!

I came to Christ in 2012. It was not easy, but I had a calling on my life. I had to renounce homosexuality, and I was not freed and delivered until 2014. During my walk with Christ, I have been continually reminded of how much goes on around us and how anything can happen at any given time and day.

On May 2, 2019, I was in a very serious car accident. I had just left my Life Group at church and was driving home in my Chevrolet Aveo when a truck rammed into me, and I, in turn, slammed into a semi-truck. I had to be cut out of the car and ended up with a broken jaw, which meant that I couldn't chew and had breathing issues. I now have a rod and two screws in my back to help me stand up straight, and nerve damage on the left side of my body. My speech and memory were affected, and I spoke much more slowly than I did before the accident. My time hosting the daily prayer line for our church and my church attendance have helped me to regain my speech and my memory. The enemy tried to take my life from behind on that expressway; and although I lost my spleen, I did not lose my God!

God is still working *on* me, *through* me, and *with* me, making me more like His beloved Son Jesus with the help of the Holy Spirit. My role is to let Him continue to do His work and to be strong, showing what I am made of and doing what He tells me to do…not so that I can boast about my achievements but to recognize that where I am and who I have become has been through the hand and power of God!

God is Creator, Lord, Savior, and Deliverer. He is worthy of my trust and praise. His Word is dependable—and for this, I can rejoice, sing, dance, and give thanks.

JoAnn LaTasha Smith-Figures

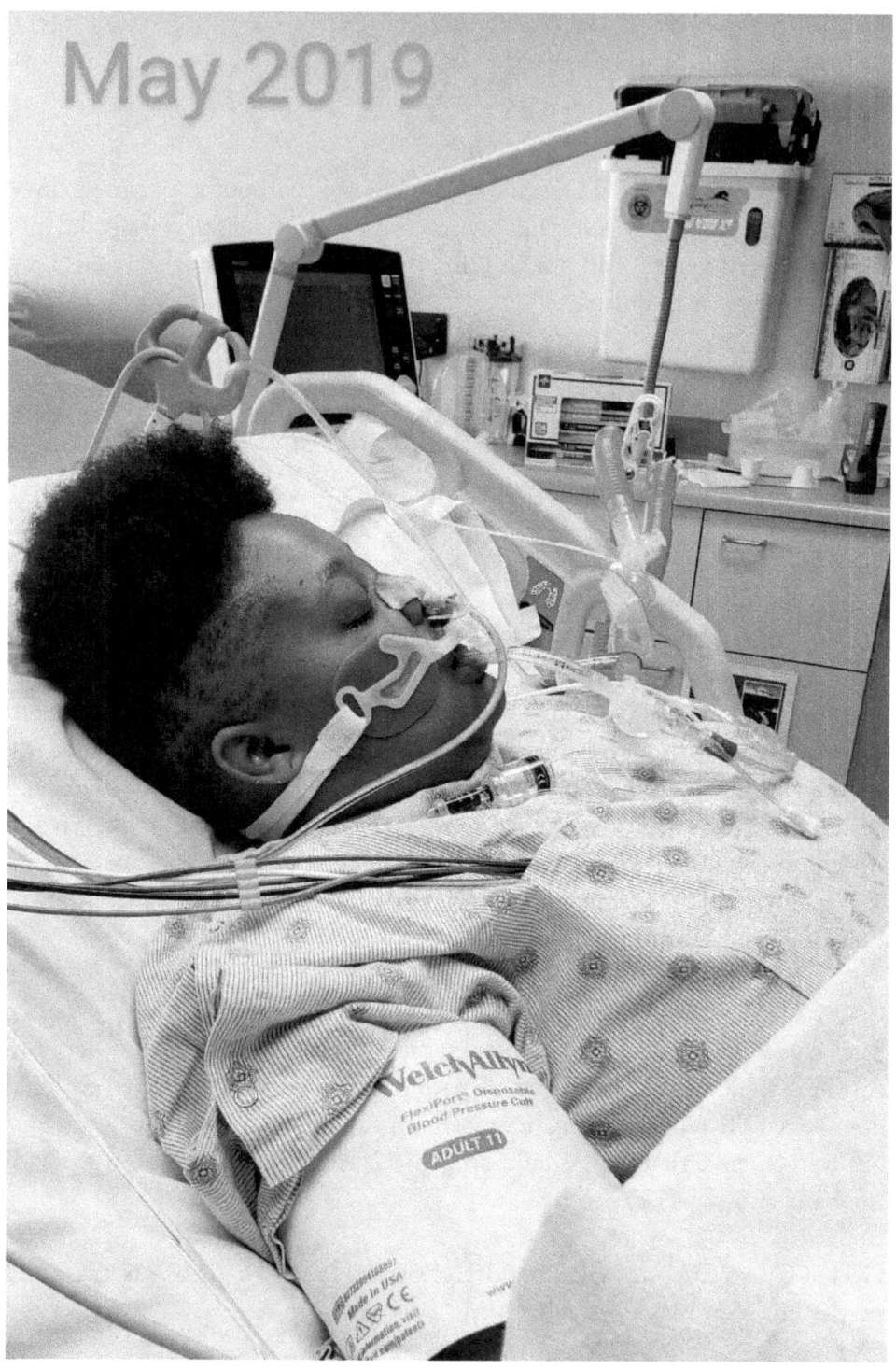

May 2019

# Prayers During A Global Crisis

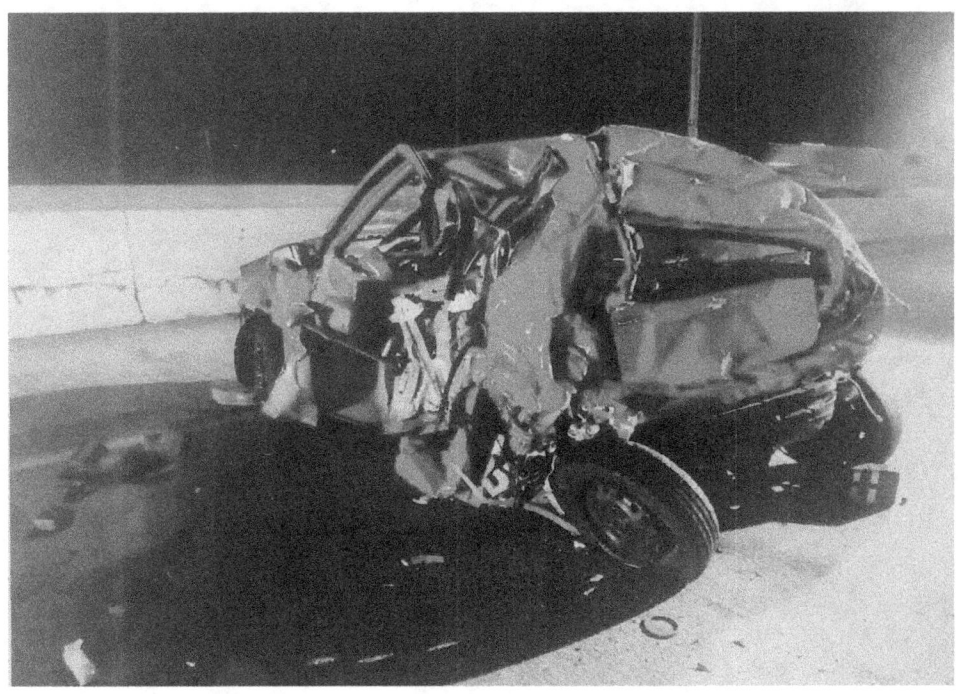

# DEDICATION

*I dedicate this book to my parents, who have shielded and protected me, and who continue to guide me through adulthood. I am forever grateful, and I thank them for the fingerprints of their love on my heart.*

# Day 1
## THANK HIM FOR WHO HE IS

Heavenly Father, thank you for who you are. We are here on earth for a purpose and a reason, and you are faithful and so worthy. Thank you for your Son. Have your way, in Jesus' name. As your people are worried and concerned, we ask you to give us clear opportunities to talk about the hope and peace found in the gospel. Please help those who are dealing with an illness during such a time as this, especially the elderly who are high-risk right now.

> *"The Lord is gracious and compassionate,*
> *slow to anger and rich in love."*
> **(Psalm 145:8 NIV)**

> *"For God so loved the world that He gave His one and only Son, that whoever believes in Him shall not perish but have eternal life."*
> **(John 3:16 NIV)**

Father God, thank you for your love and for adoring us the way you do. Thank you that your love is not static or self-centered; it reaches out and draws others in. Thank you for paying for our sins through the life of your Son…who paid the highest price that He could pay. Hallelujah! Lord, if there is someone reading this who has never trusted Christ, let this promise of everlasting life be theirs, and I pray that they believe.

> *"If you declare with your mouth, 'Jesus is Lord,' and believe in your heart that God raised him from the dead, you will be saved. For it is with your heart that you believe and are justified, and it is with your mouth that you profess your faith and are saved. As Scripture says, 'Anyone who believes in him will never be put to shame.' For there is no difference between Jew and Gentile—the same Lord is Lord of all and richly blesses all who call on him, for, 'Everyone who calls on the name of the Lord will be saved.'"*
> ***(Romans 10:9-13 NIV)***

Father God, we know that it is not a complicated process. If we simply believe and say with our mouth that Christ is the risen Lord, we will be saved. We know that hard times will come, but we also know that you keep your promises, and you will never fail to provide for us.

> *"Carry each other's burdens, and in this way, you will fulfill the law of Christ."*
> ***(Galatians 6:2 NIV)***

Lord, help us to never give in or give up, because we all need help sometimes. No one should be excused from the task of helping others. The Body of Christ functions best when its members work together for the common good.

> *"Is anyone of you in trouble? He should pray. Is anyone happy? Let him sing songs of praise. Is anyone of you sick? He should call the elders of the church to pray over him and anoint him with oil, in the name of the Lord. And the prayer offered in faith will make the sick person well; the Lord will raise him up. If he has sinned, he will be forgiven."*
> ***(James 5:13-15 NIV)***

Father God, all prayers are subject to your will and are part of your healing process. We are not alone, and we should be able to count on each other as members of Christ's body for support and prayer, especially with everything that is going on in our world…but you can carry any load for us, in Jesus' name.

*"And if you spend yourselves on behalf of the hungry and satisfy the needs of the oppressed, then your light will rise in the darkness, and your night will become the noonday."*
***(Isaiah 58:10 NIV)***

Lord, I pray that we let our service go beyond our own personal growth to include acts of kindness, charity, justice, and generosity. I pray that we will keep applying your Word to our society, and to your people. Thank you for guiding us. We give you all of our burdens, because we know that you will take care of us. You made us, and we are yours. Thank you for who you are. We pray all this in the name of Jesus. Amen.

# Day 2
## THANK HIM FOR UNITY IN THE SPIRIT

Thank you, Lord, for this amazing, wonderful day that you have made. We glorify, honor, and appreciate you. With everything that is going on, we can lose our focus…but we must put you first. Let us be thankful and grateful for all you have provided us with…our family, our loved ones, and the time that we all have been given to spend together. God, you woke us up today, and we are alive and blessed. We apologize for complaining, as we know that there are those who did not wake up this morning; but for those of us who did, I pray that we are healthy and of good courage.

We know that we are not alone; we should be able to count on each other as members of Christ's body for prayer and support, especially in times such as these. We ask you, Lord, to carry our burdens.

> *"Finally, brothers and sisters, rejoice! Strive for full restoration, encourage one another, be of one mind, live in peace. And the God of love and peace will be with you."*
> **(2 Corinthians 13:11 NIV)**

Let our service go beyond our own personal growth to include acts of kindness, charity, justice, and generosity, and help us to keep applying your work to your people.

You are in control of everything that happens in this world, and nothing can happen without your approval. Help us to keep your commands no matter what we see. For *"we walk by faith, not by sight."* Let this be a year of elevation, spiritual growth, freedom, great wealth, and health. We need our eyes to stay focused on you, Lord Jesus, and we need our souls to be filled with the power of the Holy Spirit. I speak this in Jesus' mighty name. Fill us with harmony, so that we can work well together and get along in our relationships with our families and friends. Wherever we go Lord, fill us with joy and peace.

> *"For we are God's handiwork, created in Christ Jesus to do good works, which God prepared in advance for us to do."*
> ***(Ephesians 2:10 NIV)***

I declare that we have your powerful creative work in us, in Jesus' name.

I pray that we honor you, Lord God, and we know that you will honor us. May your angels watch over us, healing the sick and helping those who are homeless or lost. Thank you for pouring out your Spirit. Help us to live so closely to you that we become restless until your will is accomplished through us, in Jesus' name.

I pray that we learn to "give you a little more time." We know your purpose and plans, and that time is short—but there is a great calling on us! Lord, remove what needs to be removed, and have your way in our lives. Your kingdom is everlasting, and it endures forever through all generations.

> *"How good and pleasant it is*
> *when God's people live together in unity!*
> *It is like precious oil poured on the head,*
> *running down on the beard,*
> *running down on Aaron's beard,*
> *down on the collar of his robe.*
> *It is as if the dew of Hermon*
> *were falling on Mount Zion.*
> *For there the Lord bestows his blessing,*
> *even life forevermore."*
> ***(Psalm 133:1-3 NIV)***

We know unity can be hard to find, but right now help us to work together as one. Help us to connect with one another, to love and support our neighbor, and to live for you because you are the King of Kings and the Lord of Lords. Unity in the church shows a positive example to the world and helps us draw together in our struggles.

Renew and elevate us so that we can get rid of the pride that keeps us from being unified. Help us with our purpose in life to work together for you, Lord. Help our outward expression of unity to reflect our inward purpose.

Your will be done on earth as it is in Heaven. You are glorious, gracious Lord.

> *"The Lord is my light and my salvation— whom shall I fear? The Lord is the stronghold of my life—of whom shall I be afraid?"*
> ***(Psalm 27:1 NIV)***

# Day 3
## THANK HIM FOR HIS LOVE

Good morning and God bless you. I believe and know that the anointing of the Lord is moving throughout this world. You can pray in your home. Pray in your car. Pray wherever you find yourself. Bask in His presence and shout. Cry out to God to release you to receive whatever He has for you this morning.

Thank you, Lord. We thank you. We glorify and magnify you. We worship, praise, and thank you for who you are. We know that you sent your only Son to die for us. We just want to say thank you so very much for thinking of each and every one of us. You are worthy, and we come before you in the name of Jesus. Forgive us for our sins that we commit before you, and help us to make right choices and decisions in life. Lead us, and guide us, Father God. Cover every business with the blood of Jesus. Help turn the minds of the wicked, and right everything that is wrong in your eyes, in Jesus' name.

Help us to love one another, looking at each person's heart to bring out the good in them. Help us to be of good courage, knowing that you are in this to help us. Cover us in the blood of Jesus. Lord, we stand in the gap, believing and knowing that our prayers are heard and answered. Thank you, Father, for using us as your vessel. Thank you for the opportunities to show your glory. Lord, we invite you today to join us in all areas of our life. We give you permission to do what you feel is best for us. Fill us with your boldness so that we can continue to tell others about you. Let our walk be a testimony to someone, so they will want to get out of whatever mess they are in. I pray for strength, peace, joy, rest, relaxation, and smiling to enter our lives, in Jesus' name.

> *"Above all, love each other deeply, because love covers a multitude of sins. Offer hospitality to one another without grumbling."*
> **(1 Peter 4:8-9 NIV)**

I pray that we will continue to live expectantly, trusting and believing in you. I pray that we are continually growing our walk with you in ministry; using whatever plans, purposes, and gifts that you have blessed us with for your kingdom. Help us to grow in love for you and for others. I pray that you will help us to invest our time and talents where they will make an eternal difference.

> *"Consider it pure joy, my brothers, whenever you face trials of many kinds because you know that the testing of your faith develops perseverance. Perseverance must finish its work so that you may be mature and complete, not lacking anything."*
> **(James 1:2-4 NIV)**

Thank you, Lord, for the joy through it all. Only you know the depths of our character until we see how we react under pressure. I pray that we are kind no matter what is going on. I pray that we put on our "love outfit" today, so that we can look like you. Help us to look like Jesus, for we know that there is power in the name of Jesus. We declare today that joy shall enter our hearts, in Jesus' mighty name.

Lord, thank you for connecting us. We give you honor and glory, because it is all you, showing up and showing out. We praise you and worship you. Thank you for being with us through trying times, for we know that they provide opportunities for us to grow. Instead of complaining about our struggles, we are looking for growth and believing that you will turn everything around for your good.

> *"In the same way, faith by itself, if it is not accompanied by action, is dead. But someone will say, 'You have faith, I have deeds.' Show me your faith without deeds and I will show you my faith by my deeds."*
> **(James 2:17-18 NIV)**

I pray that by our actions, we will show that our commitment to you is real. Let us have verification of our faith in Christ. True faith involves a commitment of our whole self to you. I know we are believing to receive from you, but we must be patient, because patience holds us until we receive what we're believing in you for. Have your way, Holy Ghost. Have your way, in Jesus' name. Amen.

## Closing prayer

Thank you, thank you. You are a good God. Lord, you gave up your Son to remove the barrier standing between you and us. Thank you for Jesus. Your desire is for us to prosper and be in good health, with a new level of faith, new realm of energy, and divine strength.

I pray and declare that we are living, walking testimonies to those around us, who are defeated by this world. Thank you for the victory and for our new life in Jesus. We declare that the world would come to know you! Protect us; bless and reach every single one of our family and friends. Lord, help us to be about the business of our Father's house and the business of salvation, where we all belong. This is exactly the business that we should all be concerned with. Help us see with Jesus' eyes our true concern and interest—eternal life with you. We thank you. We love you, Lord, and we pray all in the wonderful and precious name of Jesus. Amen.

> *"Before I formed you in the womb, I knew you, before you were born, I set you apart; I appointed you as a prophet to the nations."*
> ***(Jeremiah 1:5 NIV)***

# Day 4
## THANK HIM FOR RELATIONSHIP

Good morning. You may enter into your place of worship, walk around, kneel, stand, shout, cry out in prayer…whatever you do in God's presence is okay to do. He sees and hears us all.

We thank you, Lord. We magnify you…we appreciate you…we glorify you, Father God, and we thank you for who you are, for we know that we are nothing without you. Our faith in you is growing continuously stronger in Jesus' mighty name. Lord, we need you. Forgive us for our sins that we commit before you Lord. For any complaining and any nonsense, Lord forgive us. Help us to repent, confess, release, and surrender whatever we try to hold on to; giving it to you Lord Jesus, because it will free us and keep us from being down when you want us to be lifted high, enjoying life and knowing that you are real.

Thank you, Lord, for reminding us not to hold on to anything that weighs us down but to cast all our worries, anxieties, and cares upon you. I pray that we let go and let you have your way in our life. You are at our side, caring for us and easing our distress. I declare that whoever is holding on to anything right now will cast it onto you, in Jesus' mighty name.

## A Word to the Believer

God will carry whatever load you have to give Him. Let it go. Jesus paid the penalty for our sins. Stop worrying. Lift your hands and shout out to God. Thank you, Father God, for your Son Jesus Christ. We can't let go of God's hand when we face rough times in our life. God has said that it's not over; we may be down, but we are not out! We have to get up and fight! God has our back…if you believe and receive that, say *"Amen!"* We can't ignore a second chance when God gives it to us. We must be thankful and know that God is in control and that He is good. God's truth remains forever, in Jesus' name. I pray that we have real family and friends that stick together in times of trouble and bring healing, love, acceptance, and understanding.

> *"Be joyful in hope, patient in affliction, faithful in prayer. Share with the Lord's people who are in need. Practice hospitality. Bless those who persecute you; bless and do not curse. Rejoice with those who rejoice; mourn with those who mourn. Live in harmony with one another. Do not be proud but be willing to associate with people of low position. Do not be conceited."*
> **(Romans 12:12-16 NIV)**

We thank you, Lord, for showing up in our lives to help us pay attention. I pray that we do not hesitate to help others that we love and know are in need during this time; and I pray that when this time is over, we still have a "love suit" filled inside our souls, in Jesus' name. Reveal to us those relationships that need to be mended so that we can lend a helping hand. Let our actions speak louder than our words.

We know that right actions lead to right feelings. Lord, we invite you into our hearts, and we thank you for giving us the peace and strength that we need to face the storms of life, in Jesus' mighty name.

## MIRACLES HAPPEN WHEN WE LET GO AND LET GOD.

> *"Now to Him who is able to do immeasurably more than all we ask or imagine, according to His power that is at work within us, to Him be glory in the church and in Christ Jesus throughout all generations, for ever and ever! Amen."*
> **(Ephesians 3:20-21 NIV)**

Thank you, Daddy God, for everything. For choosing us to be Christ's representatives on earth, in light of truth. I declare that we will live our lives worthy of the calling that we have received, because it is an awesome privilege to be called Christ's very own. I pray that we will be humble, gentle, patient, understanding, and peaceful, in Jesus' precious name.

Thank you for the overwhelming care that you have for us, Daddy God. We love you and know that you are in control and are ruler *over* all, *through* all, and *in* all, in the wonderful name of Jesus Christ. Thank you for the unity in the Body of Christ and help us to *"make every effort to keep the unity of the spirit through the bond of peace,"* in Jesus' name. *(Ephesians 4:3 NIV)*

# Closing Prayer

*"One God and Father of all, who is over all and through all and in all."*
***(Ephesians 4:6 NIV)***

God shows His active presence in the world and in the lives of believers! Thank you, *thank you*, **thank you**, Lord God. You are a good God. Thank you for Jesus. Thank you for our brothers and sisters in Christ. For our families. Thank you for the connection…the unity…the blessings that you provide for us. We receive a new level of love, growth, health, faith, and a new realm of energy and peace and strength, in Jesus' mighty name. Thank you, Jesus, that all our sins—past, present, and future—are paid for.

Perfection is for you, wisdom of God! You are next for a miracle.

I pray that we continue to stay encouraged. Reach out, touch base, and contact one another. We need to know that we are in this together. Let go of your pride or shame, and know that you have help and that we all care. God is in the midst of us. I love you. Stay encouraged.

God bless you. Have a wonderful, joyful, relaxed, peaceful day, in Jesus' name. Amen.

# Day 5
## Thank Him for the Holy Spirit

We thank you, Lord! We honor, glorify, and appreciate you! Have your way, and move by your spirit.

Good morning on this wonderful day that the Lord has made! Rejoice on this day because giants are being slain, and wondrous blessings are provided. The love of God is showing, and it has been amazing…connecting us and uniting us, even through our challenges. God is in the midst of us and still working, using us for His glory.

Jesus, you are the reason for the season. You are the reason for everything. You shed your blood for us. Thank you, Jesus. Father God, have your way. We love you. We know you are dwelling within us, changing us. I pray that we set our hearts on you, because we need a move. When things are bad, fill us with a declaration, setting our hearts and eyes on you.

## A Word to the Believer

Because the Holy Spirit dwells in us, in Jesus' name, we are growing on a personal, church, and kingdom level. I pray…I **declare**…that volunteers, leaders, and members will continue to be spirit-led. That the power of God will be manifested in His presence through us, in Jesus' mighty name. God is challenging all of us to see if we are faithful servants.

Continue to open our eyes, Lord, to know that you are shaping us to serve you in endless hope. I pray that we seek your face and not your hands. We are your sons and daughters, expecting to be shaped like you and serve you. On our bad days, we **seek** you. On our good days, we **thank** you. And on our great days, we **praise** you. We know that we need you every day. Thank you for always being here for us, in Jesus' mighty name.

Lord, I pray and declare that we will never stop praying, because we know miracles happen every day. We will never stop believing, because you can change things so quickly in our lives and in the world.

> *"Do you not know? Have you not heard? The Lord is the everlasting God, the Creator of the ends of the earth. He will not grow tired or weary and His understanding no one can fathom."*
> ***(Isaiah 40:28 NIV)***

This verse right here should take some weight off of us and lift us up, because God will not grow tired or weary. He is in control. We need to keep walking by faith and not by what we have been seeing and hearing. I pray that we are not afraid, and that we will stand firm. We *will* see the miracles, the deliverance and so much more that God will do to bring us through our day. The Lord is fighting for us. We need to be still and patient, and trust that God will protect us because He is behind us, right with each of us. He is with every leader, the government, and all of those who are in control of the choices and decisions that need to be made.

I pray Lord that we are patient; every pastor, minister, prophet, evangelist… we must be still, courageous, and confident that you are clearing a new path for us, in the mighty name of Jesus Christ.

God is transforming the panic to peace, because we cannot worry about those needs that He promises to supply.

> *"For the word of the Lord is right and true; He is faithful in all He does. The Lord loves righteousness and justice; the earth is full of His unfailing love."*
> ***(Psalm 33:4-5 NIV)***

God's Word can be trusted! The Bible is reliable because unlike people, God does not lie or forget. He doesn't change His words or leave His promises unfulfilled. We can trust the Bible because it contains the words of a trustworthy and unchangeable God! Hallelujah!

> *"Follow God's example, therefore, as dearly loved children and walk in the way of love, just as Christ loved us and gave himself up for us as a fragrant offering and sacrifice to God."*
> ***(Ephesians 5:1-2 NIV)***

Thank you, Jesus. Hallelujah! Father, I pray that we are imitators of Christ no matter what. Allow our love to be the same as that of Christ. We must put on our "love suit," a love that goes beyond affection to self-sacrificing service. Thank you for who you are. Lord, we love and glorify you, and praise you, in Jesus' name. Amen.

## Closing prayer

Thank you, Lord. We come into agreement with you, knowing that when two or three are gathered in your name, you are in the midst of them all.

I just want to say that I love you and pray that you stay encouraged. I pray and declare that we will thrive in this time, that we will take a turn for the better. We will become a stronger team and begin to flourish, connected and united together, in Jesus' name. I declare and speak a powerful, safe, strong, compassionate love and service to one another! Jesus is the foundation of our life.

> *"But those who hope in the Lord will renew their strength. They will soar on wings like eagles; they will run and not grow weary; they will walk and not be faint."*
> ***(Isaiah 40:31 NIV)***

We have to remember that even the strongest people get tired at times, but God's power and strength never diminish! He is never too tired or too busy to help and listen to us and we can call upon Him to renew our strength, expecting and knowing that He will help us to rise above life's distractions and difficulties. Stay encouraged. God is with us, helping, protecting, and growing us all in His kingdom. Trust and keep your faith in Jesus.

# Day 6
## PRAISE HIM FOR UNDERSTANDING

Lord, I come before you in the name of Jesus your Son, who died for our sins. Thank you for another day. Thank you for breathing into us again. This is the day that you have made, so we are going to rejoice no matter what is in front of us. Lord, let freedom ring on this day. I will not fear, because your Word says that you do not give us a spirit of fear but of a sound mind which surpasses all understanding that will guard our hearts and minds. We are going to praise you for who you are and thank you for what you are doing and have done.

Heavenly Father, lead and guide us on this day. There are many trials before us that we are facing; but we know that nothing is impossible as long as we believe and walk by faith. You said that when we have faith, it pleases you. Lord, we need you to be in the midst of us and help us to keep our faith with our eyes fixed on you and not on the challenges and obstacles that are in front of us.

> WE ARE HERE FOR YOU, LORD.
> COME AND DO WHAT YOU DO.

Today we ask that you give us strength; that we would be of one mind, one body, and one accord. That from this day on, we will build and encourage one another, taking what the devil means for evil and turning it into our good, in Jesus' name.

Lord, we ask in the name of Jesus that you dismiss the results of the test from those doctors into your report, the report of the Lord, that no matter what the results are, we will still give you the glory you deserve. Father God, we are going to be firmly planted in you because we know nothing can uproot us with you by our side. Jesus, you are the Way, the Truth, and the Life. Father God, today we ask that you take our minds captive, reminding us to think positively and to pray about everything. Lord, we cast all our cares, worries, and burdens upon you, because your yoke is easy. Renew our minds today, and fill it with peace and joy of the Lord. We thank you for wholeness and completeness in Jesus.

> **HAVE YOUR WAY LORD.
> BE WHO YOU ARE,
> AND DO WHAT YOU DO.**

We thank you in advance and give you glory, all in the name of Jesus Christ.

> *"Now may the God of peace, who through the blood of the eternal covenant brought back from the dead our Lord Jesus, that great Shepherd of the sheep, equip you with everything good for doing his will, and may he work in us what is pleasing to him, through Jesus Christ, to whom be glory for ever and ever. Amen."*
> **(Hebrews 13:20-21 NIV)**

Father God, continue to work in us and make us the kind of people that would please you. Change us from within, and enable us to help others. I pray that we trust in you and not let anything come between us and Jesus. He is sufficient and superior. I declare that we will center our lives on you, Lord Jesus.

> *"Forget the former things;*
> *do not dwell on the past.*
> *See, I am doing a new thing!*
> *Now it springs up; do you not perceive it?*
> *I am making a way in the wilderness*
> *and streams in the wasteland."*
> **(Isaiah 43:18-19 NIV)**

Our past miracles were nothing compared to what God will do for His children in the future. Hallelujah!

In a changing world, we can trust our unchanging Lord. We have to be still and know that He is God. I declare that we will not hesitate to receive joy from Jesus. Thank you, Lord, for who you are. We love you; we honor and magnify you, because you are so good. Let us not worry but look to you, in Jesus' name. Father God, we are anchored in you. Have your way on this day. Fill us with peace, love, joy, and goodness, and help us to always be patient when we pray, knowing that you are right here in your timing, not ours. Thank you, God, that your love endures forever.

> *"But the fruit of the spirit is love, peace, patience, kindness,*
> *goodness, faithfulness, gentleness and self-control.*
> *Against such things there is no law."*
> **(Galatians 5:22-23 NIV)**

Father God, just as we are joined with you, I pray this whole world would turn and accept Christ into their lives. We must always know you, love you, remember you, and imitate you. I declare that every individual will turn from their sinful nature and be set free, knowing that you are who you say you are.

Let us boast about the cross of our Lord Jesus Christ. I declare that in due time, we will reap a harvest of blessing, in Jesus' mighty name. We thank you and appreciate you. We love and honor you, Father God. You are gracious and the light of our lives, in Jesus' name.

# Closing prayer

> *"Obey your leaders and submit to their authority. They keep watch over you as men who must give an account. Obey them so that their work will be a joy, not a burden, for that would be of no advantage to you. Pray for us. We are sure that we have a clear conscience and desire to live honorably in every way. I particularly urge you to pray so that I may be restored to you soon."*
> **(Hebrews 13:17-19 NIV)**

Father, I pray that we recognize the need for prayer! I rebuke the lies and schemes that Satan uses to try and destroy our work for you, when he is a liar from the pits of hell, and you are the King of Kings, the Lord of Lords, and the light of our salvation. Whom shall we fear when you go before us? *Nothing* can be against us, in Jesus' mighty name.

I pray that we remain encouraged, connected, and united, knowing that if we ever need to talk, need food, need anything, we can reach out and never feel ashamed. God loves us and wants us to be a blessing. To those that are in need, Father God, I speak greatness and motivation to take place on this day. Thank you for showing us how to be responsible for our health. It's all about you, and we thank you Lord. Have your way on this day. We pray this in Jesus' name. Amen.

# Day 7
## A PRAYER FOR GODLY LEADERS

Thank you, Father God. We love and appreciate you. Thank you for drawing near to us. You say when two or three are gathered together in your name, you are in the midst. Lord, it doesn't matter if we are physically distant because we are all spiritually connected, in Jesus' mighty name.

- Leaders in our country
- President
- Governors
- Mayors
- Pastors

Father, we know no one is perfect, and we should not judge. We lift up the president before you, asking that you would help him to make the right decisions and to know what's going on. All Christians should be people of prayer, and whether we voted for him or not, he deserves our prayers. We pray that he would be given wisdom and knowledge. Help him to remain healthy and safe, and to uphold a strong standard of righteousness in our country.

> "For he is God's servant to do you good. But if you do wrong be afraid, for he does not bear the sword for nothing. He is God's servant, an agent of wrath to bring punishment on the wrongdoer."
> ***(Romans 13:4 NIV)***

Lord, we know if we are doing right, we have nothing to fear, and we also know that you are in control. We declare that our president will pursue peace and prosperity for America, in Jesus' name. We lift him up to do everything in his power to continue to care for those who need assistance and to execute justice for all people.

> *"Do not pervert justice, do not show partiality to the poor or favoritism to the great, but judge your neighbor fairly."*
> ***(Leviticus 19:15 NIV)***

Lord, we know that we are to follow all of your laws. Please help our president improve the lives of those he has been blessed to lead. We decree and declare that he will do what is best for all of us. We pray that he will lead America to continue to be a light for all nations, in Jesus' mighty name, and I pray that he will walk humbly with you.

I pray that you would help all of our leaders to identify the needs of your people through divine wisdom and understanding. Help them to be effective leaders and to act for the betterment of your kingdom, in Jesus' name. We thank you, God, for who you are. You are amazing and so gracious and righteous to use us to come into agreement for our country. Father God, give our leaders a soft hand and a stiff backbone. Give them a quiet determination that marches toward justice no matter what they are facing. Let them be *"as wise as serpents and innocent as doves."*

> *"The Lord gives strength to His people; the Lord blesses His people with peace."*
> ***(Psalm 29:11 NIV)***

Father, in the name of Jesus Christ, release peace into the hearts of our pastors and strengthen their minds and bodies, in your name and through your power. Father God, we pray against worry and ask that you will protect them from stress and anxiety, in Jesus' name. Help our pastors to walk in their purpose, knowing that your hand is upon them. Give them the confidence to do your works with your mighty authority.

Lord God, grant them peace of mind and calm their troubled hearts. Declare balance for them to receive and not to stumble or worry, because you are in control. I pray that they would receive strength and clarity of mind to find their purpose and walk the path you have laid out for them. They are shepherding your people, so fill them with a "love suit," gladden their hearts, and bring peace to their souls.

Help our pastors to learn and to focus on what they are learning. Remind them to trust themselves. Ease their expectations, and guide them to open up to someone they trust. Show them how to move toward something instead of away, then take a few steps back and give themselves time to process.

We declare today that every pastor shall take a deep breath and release their burdens. What is going on in our lives right now does not mean that God is not powerful, real, or unstoppable. We must be patient and still, recognizing that everything is all in God's timing, in Jesus' mighty name.

We know that God has revealed His power through mighty miracles over nature, and we know that He promises to continue to reveal His power.

Remember that God gives us strength. The power that controls creation and raises the dead is available to us, in Jesus' precious name. Amen.

> *"Truly he is my rock and my salvation; he is my fortress; I will not be shaken. My salvation and my honor depend on God; he is my mighty rock, my refuge. Trust in him at all times, you people; pour out your hearts to him, for God is our refuge."*
> **(Psalm 62:6-8 NIV)**

> *"Because your love is better than life, my lips will glorify you. I will praise you as long as I live, and in your name, I will lift up my hands. I will be fully satisfied as with the richest of foods; with singing lips my mouth will praise you."*
> **(Psalm 63:3-5 NIV)**

# Day 8
## PRAISE HIM FOR FREEDOM

Thank you, Lord. Thank you, Heavenly Father, for you are a good God; gracious, worthy, and faithful. I come into agreement with my brothers and sisters, for we know that you are in the midst when two or three are gathered in your name. Father in heaven, today I pray that we will choose to release everything that has tried to hold us back. Today is a new day, with new joy and new transformation every time we are in your presence.

Lift your hands and say, *"I release the past. I release bitterness, failure, and missed opportunities."* I pray that we will embrace your grace and power to boldly move forward into the blessings you have for us, in Jesus' name. We are a beautiful reflection of God. We are loved and forgiven. We have been redeemed. I pray that we let go and let God have His way.

Lord God, you desire for us to live in freedom and never intended for us to live in bondage or fear. We thank you Lord for not putting any fear in us because your Word says, *"Whom shall I fear that you are the strength of my life."* **(Psalm 27:1 NIV)** Thank you for giving us the weapons we need for victory; weapons with divine power to demolish strongholds and the lies and works of the enemy. Lord Jesus, destroy arguments and every bit of pride that keeps us from knowing you more. Take our every thought captive, and make us obedient to Christ.

> *"For though we live in the world, we do not wage war as the world does. The weapons we fight with are not the weapons of the world. On the contrary, they have divine power to demolish*

> *strongholds. We demolish arguments and every pretension that sets itself up against the knowledge of God and we take captive every thought to make it obedient to Christ. And we will be ready to punish every act of disobedience, once your obedience is complete."*
> **(2 Corinthians 10:3-6 NIV)**

Our God is a *"way maker, miracle worker, promise keeper and light in the darkness."* (Leeland. CD. Way Maker, 2019.)

Hallelujah! Praise God! We gotta choose to use God's methods and not the world's. God's methods are prayer, faith, hope, love, His Word, the Holy Spirit, and all that is so powerful and effective, in Jesus' name. These methods will break down the walls that Satan builds to keep us from finding God.

Right now, we rebuke every lie from Satan. We come against the lies right now, in the precious name of Jesus Christ. I pray that we never try to use our own methods, but always use God's methods, because nothing can break down these barriers. Thank you, Father God, for your amazing promises…your amazing steps that you provide us with. We love you. We magnify you. We honor you… because without you, we can do nothing. I pray that we will remain patient and still, knowing that you are in control of everything and keeping our faith in you. You are the Head and the Maker of this whole world, and we are blessed. You have united us all together night and day, and everything is going to be alright because we are not alone. You are with us and will never fail us.

> *"This is what the Lord says—Israel's King and Redeemer, the Lord Almighty: 'I am the first and I am the last; apart from me there is no God. Who then is like me? Let him proclaim it. Let him declare and lay out before me what has happened since I established my ancient people, and what is yet to come—yes, let them foretell what will come. Do not tremble, do not be afraid. Did I not proclaim this and foretell it long ago? You are my witnesses. Is there any God besides me? No, there is no other Rock; I know not one.'"*
> **(Isaiah 44:6-8 NIV)**

Thank you, Father God, for you are good. I pray that we are proud of belonging to you, and that we are unashamed and delighted to let everyone know about our relationship with our Father. We praise and appreciate you, for we have victory and new life in you.

*"No, there is no other Rock; I know not one."* Hallelujah! Our God is not impressed by money, fame, and power; we can't deceive ourselves and empower our lives. We have to look to Him, for there is only one true God.

If our God can...

- Put Jesus in the fiery furnace with Shadrach, Meshach, and Abednego...
- Close the lion's mouth for Daniel...
- Part the Red Sea for Moses...
- Make the sun stand still for Joshua...
- Open the prison doors for Peter...
- Put a baby in Sarah's arms...
- Raise Lazarus from the dead...

*Then He can certainly take care of us!*

God has everything under control!

It's not about stopping all the things that look bad; it's about *who's in there with us*!

We are the chosen, just like Israel, and we don't have anything to worry about.

> *"But you are a chosen people, a royal priesthood, a holy nation, God's special possession, that you may declare the praises of him who called you out of darkness into his wonderful light."*
> **(1 Peter 2:9 NIV)**

# Day 9
## PRAISE HIM FOR THE VICTORY

Today, Father, we thank you. We magnify you, glorify you, and honor you. Lord, we just say, "thank you," and we know that you are in control. We know that we have to trust you and relax, pray, grow, and help one another… because we have no other choice! We come in agreement because we know you are in the midst when two or three are gathered. As we sit, stand, kneel, shout, and hold hands quietly in your presence, shine your peace into our troubled world. Assure us that we do not have to live in defeat.

In you, Lord God, we can have peace and victory, knowing that when troubles come, it is you wanting to get us off the wrong path and focused on you. That when we look up, things begin to change in our lives. When we trust in you, good news always comes. Lord, free us from these shackles and lift us up above our circumstances. Help us to rest in your presence, receiving the joy that no one can take away from us and keeping our eyes fixed on you no matter what comes our way. Thank you for the fellowship, relationship, and discipleship that is taking place during these trying times. Thank you for the bonding that is happening in homes, at work, and wherever we are traveling. Father, there is so much transformation happening.

We know that you are bigger than whatever crisis we face, and that you are our shield of protection, in Jesus' name. We thank you and appreciate you.

> *"I have given you authority to trample on snakes and scorpions and to overcome all the power of the enemy; nothing will harm you. However, do not rejoice that the spirits submit to you, but rejoice that your names are written in heaven."*
> **(Luke 10:19-20 NIV)**

Thank you, Jesus, for helping us to get our priorities right during these stressful times. Let us remember that our names were written in heaven before the creation of the world. Thank you that we are seeing your wonders at work in and through us, ensuring that we do not lose sight of the greatest wonder of all, which is our heavenly citizenship in Jesus Christ. Hallelujah! Praise you, God!

Lord God, we ask that you continue to keep us firm in the hope you have set before us, so that we shall be set free, and the whole world will live to praise your name, through Christ, our Lord and Savior. Thank you for the grace of Jesus. We ask that the love of God and the fellowship of the Holy Spirit be with us, in Jesus' name.

Help us to not just talk, but to put action into what we are believing for, because you have empowered us to be all that you called and chose us to be. Lead us and guide us, because we know that faith without works is dead, and only you can transform us in your presence.

Your love makes it worth it all. Thank you for your presence that is taking place right now in the atmosphere. Have your way, in Jesus' name.

Father God, we thank you for keeping your word concerning your promises toward us. Thank you for your loving kindness even at a time such as this.

Lord, I bring all of this before your throne today. The sickness, panic attacks, the downcast, and all who are in urgent need. We stand in the gap for the infants who cry out in pain. Lord Jehovah, you know that those who are sick and in pain are sometimes unable to speak or even pray for themselves. May your grace and healing power come upon them, in the precious wonderful name of Jesus. Lord give grace to the elderly, the poor, and the homeless. Defend the orphans and widows who through no fault of their own have become victims. Abba Father, hear us from heaven and heal our land. Revive our spirits, and let our prayers and petitions be acceptable before your sight, in Jesus' mighty name.

Thank you, Father, for who you are. We have been stamped by you, which means we are *blessed*. Hallelujah! What God has spoken and declared over us cannot be reversed…because it is irreversible!

We are family, and we are in this thing together.

> *"Just as a body, though one, has many parts, but all its many parts form one body, so it is with Christ. For we were all baptized by one Spirit so as to form one body—whether Jews or Gentiles, slave or free—and we were all given the one Spirit to drink."*
> ***(1 Corinthians 12:12-13 NIV)***

Family, we have one thing in common, and that's our faith in Christ. We have been finding and embracing unity, and I pray…I *declare*…that we will continue to use the gifts that we have been given and encourage others to use theirs, in Jesus' name.

I pray that we get involved in the lives of others, not only our own enjoyable walk with God but reaching out and helping others, in Jesus' name.

Our spiritual gifts are beneficial when we use them to help everyone in the church and to communicate God's message, providing insight, warning, correction, and encouragement.

> *"Now you are the body of Christ and each of you is a part of it."*
> ***(1 Corinthians 12:27 NIV)***

# Day 10
## THANK HIM FOR HIS STRENGTH

*Heavenly Father*, we thank you. We glorify, honor, love, and appreciate you. We choose to rejoice in you no matter what, because we trust that you are in control. Forgive us for the sins that we commit before you. Thank you for your forgiveness, Lord God. I pray that the world would seek you and turn to you; knowing that you do not look at our past and that you see greatness in us.

I pray that we would realize how special we are in your eyes. Thank you, Father, that when we kneel in your presence, no one can stand against us, in Jesus' name. Our plans may change but your purpose never fails. I declare that we would make a choice; a decision to always have faith in our Abba Father, because when we look up to you, things begin to change, and we feel peace like never before.

Abba, thank you for your Son Jesus, who died for us in our place, because He loved us and wanted us to be able to return and live with Him and regain our bodies. Thank you, Jesus, for volunteering, knowing that your suffering was necessary and that only a perfect being could satisfy justice for all the wrongdoing in the world.

Father, thank you for who you are and for what you are doing in our lives. I pray that this whole nation…this whole *world*…would accept Christ and be born again. I pray that we would repent, renounce, confess, and surrender during these trying times, knowing that surrender and repentance leads to eternal life, in Jesus' name, and that no unclean thing can inherit the kingdom of God.

Help us to reach out to those who are struggling and may be lost because of what is going on. They may not know how to understand your Word or get into your presence. They may not realize that we can make our homes into a place of praise and worship.

> *"As for God, His way is perfect; the word of the Lord is flawless. He is a shield for all who take refuge in Him."*
> **(Psalm 18:30 NIV)**

> *"He gives His king great victories; He shows unfailing kindness to His anointed, to David and His descendants forever."*
> **(Psalm 18:50 NIV)**

Thank you, Abba Father, for being our shield. Help us to reach out and help those who are weak and having a hard time making it on their own. You chose us to help those who are in need. Lord, you don't want us to remain weak. Thank you for the strength, protection, and guidance that you give us when we are fighting the evil in the world…but when *you* fight our battles, we have nothing to worry about! I pray…I *declare*…that we will never be cowards. We are mighty warriors because only God could ultimately protect and save us, in Jesus' name. God gives us the victory in every battle.

Father, we know that all things will be restored to their proper and perfect frame, in Jesus' mighty name. Help us not to return to the same stuff that we used to do. Let us continue to grow and transform everything that you have been doing during this time, where we are fully cooperating with everything that has been changed due to these tough circumstances. Thank you for lighting a fire in your people. Some may have noticed that you have been seeing through our falsehoods and emptiness from the beginning. You want to get our attention and bring a transforming walk of power to explode your house. I know (and I pray others know) that you are not finished. We can still pray, teach, minister, evangelize, prophesy, disciple, mentor, and preach, even when we are not physically together. Remaining spiritually connected is what you have called and chosen us to do, in Jesus' name. We thank you, Lord God.

> *"They will be my people, and I will be their God. I will give them singleness of heart and action, so that they will always fear me for their own good and the good of their children after them. I will make an everlasting covenant with them: I will never stop doing good to them and I will inspire them to fear me, so that they will never turn away from me. I will rejoice in doing them good and will assuredly plant them in this land with all my heart and soul."*
> ***(Jeremiah 32:38-41 NIV)***

Hallelujah!

Thank you, God, for your promises…*Yes* and *Amen!*

Thank you for using your power to accomplish your purpose through your people. Give us the power to be all that you want us to be, not who we want to be. Thank you for opening our eyes to see the responsibility and priorities that you want us to change and transform. Have your way above all else, in Jesus' name. Amen.

# Closing Prayer

Thank you, Abba Father, for everything. We are blessed and highly favored. Continue to strengthen our faith and our trust in you, knowing that we are not alone. Thank you for helping us to stay connected and united, reaching out and going above and beyond in times of crisis. We are spiritually connected and not worried about the lies and works of the enemy. We are growing and moving forward in the kingdom of God, setting examples and walking in victory. We are walking testimonials of what you are restoring, redeveloping, and recreating in our lives, in Jesus' name.

I pray that we continue to push and press our way during this season, because you are behind the scenes, guiding us with your Word, even if we don't see you. I declare and speak that we will be stronger, wiser, and so much better after this test, in Jesus' mighty name. Amen.

> DO NOT LET WHAT YOU **SEE** CAUSE YOU TO FORGET ABOUT WHAT GOD HAS **SAID**. CONTINUE TO SERVE GOD FAITHFULLY AND MAKE JESUS THE KING OF YOUR LIFE. WORSHIP HIM AS YOUR SAVIOR, KING, AND LORD.

*"And teaching them to obey everything I have commanded you. And surely, I am with You always, to the very end of the age."*
***(Matthew 28:20 NIV)***

# Day 11
## Praise Him for His Glory

Father God, we give you thanks and praise that when we were still far-off, you met us in your Son and brought us home. Dying and loving, He declared your love, gave us grace, and opened the gate of glory. May we who share Christ's body live His risen life to others; may we whom the Spirit lights give light to the world. Jesus, only your life in us can empower us to face an endless flow of problems with good cheer. Keep us firm in the hope you have set before us, so that all of your children shall be free, and the whole earth will live to praise your name, through Christ our Lord. Help us to lay everything down. Wrap us in your arms and take us to that secret place in you. Lead us and guide us, in Jesus' name.

As we sit quietly in your presence, shine your peace into our troubled minds and hearts. Little by little, free us from earthly shackles, and lift us above our circumstances. Help us to rest in your presence, receiving the joy that no one can take away from us. Jesus, help us to keep our eyes fixed on you. May the grace of the Lord Jesus Christ, the love of God, and the fellowship of the Holy Spirit be with us always and forever.

> PRAYER IS NOT A WAY FOR **US** TO CONTROL **GOD**...IT IS A WAY FOR US TO PUT OURSELVES **UNDER GOD'S CONTROL**.

Lord, we thank you for prayer, our direct line to you. I declare that the responsibility of every Christian is to remember that everything is in God's situation, purpose, time, and place. Asking God to do His will blesses, protects, and brings favor in our lives. Miracles happen when God moves. Without prayer, we would wither and faint. "

> *"Rejoice always, pray continually, give thanks in all circumstances; for this is God's will for you in Christ Jesus."*
> **(1 Thessalonians 5:16-18 NIV)**

Thank you, Father God, for your promises that fill us with joy, peace, and strength. When we do your will, it is easier to be joyful and thankful.

Lord, you are so amazing, worthy, and faithful. Abba, we love you for who you are.

Lord, we know that storms are only temporary, but your blessings last forever. Arm us with strength, peace, and love. Humble us, and help us to be patient and still and to trust in your timing.

You make our way perfect. We need you, Abba Father, because you will work out your perfect plan, in Jesus' mighty name.

Abba, we thank you that when troubles arise, it is necessary for your manifestation to take place in our lives. I declare that we will go from the pit to the palace just as Joseph did. There are many blessings that you have waiting for us on the other side of the trials that we go through. The trials are meant to destroy us, but they will turn out to be in our favor. Thank you, Jesus. I believe that trials and storms come because you want to build, develop, and strengthen our faith and determination.

Father God, we all experience times of joy and times of pain, times where we feel close to you, and times where we feel distant. Even in the times of spiritual drought or circumstantial pain, we know that you are calling us to seek you. Thank you, Lord, that through prayer and reading your Word, we can find the answers to overcome these obstacles. Thank you, Jesus, for being far above everything that tries to hinder us.

> *"He gave you manna to eat in the desert, something your Fathers had never known, to humble and to test you so that in the end it might go well with you. You may say to yourself, 'My power and the strength of my hands have produced this wealth for me.' But remember the Lord your God, for it is He who gives you the ability to produce wealth and to confirm His covenant, which He swore to your forefathers as it is today."*
> **(Deuteronomy 8:16-18 NIV)**

You are so gracious and good, Father God. Thank you for wrapping your arms around us and embracing us through it all. Thank you for helping us not to push you out of our lives during a time like this. It is easy to prioritize other things in life during the storms, but this is when you get our attention to embrace what makes us uncomfortable and become unstoppable, in Jesus' name. Thank you that during this struggle, you have been turning it around for your goodness and glory, providing for us a better land. You have allowed hardship in our lives to bring us through to a better place. Hallelujah!

Thank you, Abba, for working around us and through us to do good. We praise you for all you have done and are yet to do in this rough season. We trust you because you are in control. I declare that we will read our Bible, pray, come into agreement to follow you, obey you, grow, and mature because that is all we can do when we know who you are in our lives. That when we don't understand or know what you are doing, we will remember who is in control. Lord, in such a time as this, there is love on display. I pray that the whole world accepts it and receives it, in the mighty name of Jesus Christ. Thank you, Abba, for giving us everything we have and helping us, guiding us to continue to manage what you called, and appointed and ordained us to do for you Lord God. We love you, Lord, and thank you in Jesus' name.

# Closing Prayer

*"Be careful to follow every command I am giving you today, so that you may live and increase, and may enter and possess the land that the Lord promised on oath to your forefathers. Remember how the Lord your God led you all the way in the desert these forty years, to humble you and to test you in order to know what was in your heart, whether or not you would keep His commands. He humbled you, causing you to hunger and then feeding you with manna, which neither you nor your father had known, to teach you that man does not live on bread alone but on every word that comes from the mouth of the Lord."*
**(Deuteronomy 8:1-3 NIV)**

Thank you, Abba Father, for helping us to be totally committed to you at such a time as this, because we know you are the One who created life itself. Life requires discipline, sacrifice, and hard work. Thank you for renewing us, and for the new realm level of faith, energy, health, peace, and divine strength that we are living. We are walking testimonials. We are not alone; we are spiritually connected in Jesus Christ. Thank you, Father. We love you and pray all this in Jesus' name. Amen.

# Day 12
## THANK HIM FOR VISION

Thank you, Lord. We worship you this day. We love you and come before you, humbling ourselves in Jesus' mighty name. We know you are who you say you are…the King of Kings and Lord of Lords. Hallelujah! We praise you and thank you for waking us up; our first blessing of the day. You breathed in us again, Lord. Thank you, thank you…for we know you are not yet finished with us. Turning to prayer is the most personal way to experience you, to encounter you, and to grow in our knowledge of you. Thank you for seeing us through and being by our side at such a time as this. You are in control, Lord.

> *"For His anger lasts only a moment, but His favor lasts a lifetime; weeping may remain for a night but rejoicing comes in the morning."*
> **(Psalm 30:5 NIV)**

Your Word is loving and powerful. I pray that when we say we have faith, that we really trust in you no matter what, to show our absolute dependence on you, Father God. I pray that we put our hearts first, seeking you before seeking anything else, because that is when we can expect your spirit to guide us. You are our highest authority and require our first allegiance.

> *"'You will seek me with all your heart. I will be found by you,' declares the Lord, 'and will bring you back from captivity. I will gather you from all the nations and places where I have banished you,' declares the Lord, 'and will bring you back to the place from which I carried you into exile.'"*
> **(Jeremiah 29:13-14 NIV)**

Thank you, Abba, for not forgetting your people. Thank you for this new beginning with a new purpose; you are turning the whole world around. You are turning us into a new people in these times of deep trouble. I believe that you may be preparing us, as you did the people of Judah, for a new beginning with you at the center, in Jesus' mighty name.

I declare according to your wise plan that we will continue to have hope and a future in Jesus Christ. I declare that we will call on you in confidence, coming into agreement and believing, trusting, and walking by faith in you. Even though these are difficult times, we will not despair. We will not lose hope because your presence is with us through the privilege of prayer and grace. Hallelujah! You can be found when we seek you wholeheartedly. No strange lands, sorrows, frustrations, or physical problems can break that communion.

We thank you for who you are. You are gracious, worthy, faithful, and amazing. We appreciate you, Lord, and are grateful that you love us so much. You are the strength of our lives, a fortress of salvation for your anointed ones, according to your Word. Father God, you are good all the time. Thank you for filling us with peace, joy, warmth, and comfort. Your Spirit dwells in us, in Jesus' name.

> *"Praise the Lord, for He has heard my cry for mercy. The Lord is my strength and my shield; my heart trusts in Him and I am helped. My heart leaps for joy and I will give thanks to Him in song. Hallelujah!"*
> **(Psalm 28:6-7 NIV)**

Thank you, Lord, that when we are together, united and connected in prayer, we have confidence that you are in the midst of us, because your Word says when two or three are gathered together in your name, you are in the midst of it all. Thank you, Jesus. With all that is going on, you are our only source of safety. Prayer is the best help when trials come our way because prayer keeps us in communion with you.

No matter what surrounds us, every encounter with you can change us. When all we want is you, we surrender all to you, in Jesus' name. I pray that we will withhold nothing and will not drag anything back with us after we release it to you at your throne, in Jesus' mighty name.

Thank you, Abba Father, that your power reveals such amazing grace. Thank you that trusting you and knowing you gives us peace and strength to weather the storms of life. How wonderful and gracious you are! Thank you, Lord, for transforming our lives and renewing our hearts; recreating your people to be who you want us to be. Remain in us Lord, and keep filling us with your Word, your goodness, your grace, and your mercy. Continue to incline your ear to us, in Jesus' name.

## Closing Prayer

Thank you, Father. We love you and thank you for embracing us today. I ask that you wrap your arms around us today and all the days of our lives, in Jesus' name.

> *"If you remain in Me and My words remain in you, ask whatever you wish, and it will be given to you."*
> ***(John 15:7 NIV)***

Lord, I pray that this verse stays in our hearts, and that if we think about doing anything apart from you that we remember ***John 15:7***. Father God, we love you and thank you for this transition that you are making in our lives, that we will keep our eyes focused and fixed on you. I declare healing, wholeness, strength, peace, favor, and victory over your people. I pray for the finances of your people, in Jesus' name. Thank you for your protection over each one of us. I pray this in Jesus' name. Amen.

# Day 13
## THANK HIM FOR COURAGE

Thank you, Father God, for who you are. We glorify you and appreciate you. You woke us up and breathed in us again; and we know…we believe… that you are not finished with us yet. Thank you for knowing us before we were formed.

> *"Before I formed you in the womb, I knew you, before you were born, I set you apart: I appointed you as a prophet to the nations."*
> ***(Jeremiah 1:5 NIV)***

Thank you for thinking of us and planning for us. We are blessed, knowing that you thought of us as valuable sons and daughters. We are your children, Abba, and you are so gracious.

Lord, we pray that you will continue to use us for whatever purpose, plan, or task you have for us because you know everything, and you are in control.

Lord, if we do not know what our gift or task is, help us not to give up. I pray to seek to fulfill the mission like other leaders, pastors, ministers, and believers who are serving in your kingdom.

We pray that we will love, obey, and serve you until your guidance becomes clearer, and that we will do what you tell us to do, in Jesus' name. Lord, help us. We do not know what to do as many have just started to attend church. Help them to remember that we are spiritually connected, and that you have not forgotten about the baby Christians, the new members. Let them know that they have nothing to worry about, because you are right here next to us. I pray that we have peace and joy no matter what goes on. You are still in control, and we know that you make a way when there is no way. Thank you for neither sleeping nor slumbering. Thank you, Jesus, for dying for us and thinking of our faces…our *names*, knowing that you were going to *"talk with us, walk with us, and tell us that we are your own." (C. Austin Miles. In the Garden, 1912. paraphrased)*

I declare that we will not worry or doubt you, Father God, because you are real, powerful, and unstoppable. We declare that we will walk by faith and not by sight and that we will continue to trust in you because you are the King of Kings and the Lord of Lords. Thank you, Abba, for being our refuge and strength. Thank you for restoring us, making all things new and binding our wounds. Have your way in Jesus' mighty name.

> *"But I will restore you to health and heal your wounds, because you are called an outcast, Zion for whom no one cares."*
> ***(Jeremiah 30:17 NIV)***

Thank you for your promises. You are amazing Abba, and we give you the glory. We are so grateful for you, for you are worthy and faithful. You're so amazing Abba. Thank you for your love. You are so good, in spite of what happens in our lives, you remain the same today, yesterday, and forever. I pray that every one of us knows and believes that there is a God who goes before us and is with us.

> *"Be on your guard; stand firm in the faith; be men of courage; be strong. Do everything in love."*
> ***(1 Corinthians 16:13-14 NIV)***

Lord God, have your way because you are in control. You know everything, and you know what is best for us. I pray that we all are on guard during times of danger; and when the enemy tries to come against our spiritual walk, I declare that we will stand firm in our faith; that we will behave courageously, be strong, and do everything with kindness and in love no matter what is going on in this world today. I declare that we will be patient and still, that we will not worry or complain, and that we will follow your commands, in Jesus' mighty name.

I come against discouragement, and I declare that we will look to you, because you are in control and will never leave us nor forsake us. You are always good. Thank you, Lord, for desiring for us to live in freedom and never intending for us to live in bondage or fear. You give us weapons that we need for victory; divine power to demolish strongholds. Lord, we plead the blood of Jesus over us. We pray that you would protect us, cover us, and keep us safe, in Jesus' name. I speak peace, strength, and joy. Thank you, Abba, for who you are. Have your way, in Jesus' name. Our help comes from you, Lord. We don't have to see it to believe, because we know it is true.

> *"Love is patient, love is kind. It does not envy, it does not boast, it is not proud. It does not dishonor others, it is not self-seeking, it is not easily angered, it keeps no record of wrongs. Love does not delight in evil but rejoices with the truth. It always protects, always trusts, always hopes, always perseveres. Love never fails. But where there are prophecies, they will cease; where there are tongues, they will be stilled; where there is knowledge, it will pass away."*
> ***(1 Corinthians 13:4-8 NIV)***

# Day 14
## PRAISE HIM AS THE SOURCE OF OUR POWER

Heavenly Father, as I come in agreement with our pastors, I thank you for being in the midst of it all. Lord, you are close to the brokenhearted.

> *"The Lord is close to the brokenhearted
> and saves those who are crushed in spirit."*
> **(Psalm 34:18 NIV)**

Thank you, Abba, for paying attention to us when we call on you. Thank you for helping us during uncertain times. We know that you hear and act on our behalf because we love you. You are faithful and gracious, and we appreciate you and honor your glory. Thank you for your promise to be close to the brokenhearted, and to be our source of power, courage and wisdom, helping us through our troubles and problems. I declare that we will never become frustrated when trouble strikes, but that we will admit we need your help and will thank you for being by our side, in Jesus' mighty name.

> *"I will extol the Lord at all times; His praise will always be on
> my lips. My soul will boast in the Lord; let the afflicted hear and
> rejoice. Glorify the Lord with me. Let us exalt His name together."*
> **(Psalm 34:1-3 NIV)**

Hallelujah! God, you are amazing and so worthy. We do not have anything to fear or worry about because you are in control, no matter what comes our way. You promise great blessings to your people, and we must remember that many of your blessings require our active participation. We gotta praise and thank you for who you are and what you are doing at such a time as this. I pray that we remember that you will deliver us from fear. You will save us out of trouble when we have called on you and sought you. I pray that we remember how you can and will guard and deliver us when we are in fear. An angel of the Lord encamps around us. I pray that we remember how you will show us your goodness when we take refuge in you.

Thank you, Father God, that when we fear you, we will lack nothing; and when we seek you, we will lack no good thing. When we are weak and hungry and seeking you, we can talk to you, and you will always listen. Thank you that your ears are attentive to our cries. Thank you for redeeming us when we take refuge in you. I pray we remember that when we take refuge in you, that we will not be condemned.

Father God, during this time, we must remember that we are *in* this world, but we are not *of* it. I pray that we are not afraid to cry out to you. I pray that we will not tell lies and that we will turn from evil; we will do good and seek peace, stay humble and serve you, and most of all…trust in you. I know and pray that we remember that we must stay obedient; doing our part by serving God, staying in intimate relationship with Him, and seeking Him because He is in control.

Father God, I pray that the world would fear you and start showing you deep respect and honor, humbling themselves before you. I declare that the world would start praising and worshiping you, in the mighty name of Jesus.

You are always good…you are good all the time. Thank you for comforting us and filling us with peace, joy, and strength. We are under the shadow of the Most High, and He is protecting us. He is so faithful and worthy. I pray that we continue to keep our eyes fixed on you, Lord Jesus, putting our trust in you alone. I pray that we know and believe that you will make things happen that we couldn't make happen on our own and know that you are supplying all our needs in such a time as this.

The best is yet to come, and this too shall pass, in Jesus' name. I declare healing, wholeness, strength, peace, favor, and victory over all. I lift up the finances of your people. The economy is not our source…*you* are our source. Our trust is in Jesus Christ. We are a victor and never a victim, in Jesus' name. I believe it and I declare it today.

> *"May God of hope fill you with all joy and peace as You trust in Him, so that you may overflow with hope by the power of the Holy Spirit."*
> ***(Romans 15:13 NIV)***

Thank you, Lord, for your glory and for what you are doing through us; we are blessed. We are spiritually connected and not alone. Thank you for never failing nor forsaking us. Shine through us wherever we go during this time, shine in the darkness. In Jesus' name, I pray. Amen.

# Day 15
## PRAISE HIM FOR HIS COVERING

Heavenly Father, thank you for who you are. You are our shield, protector, stronghold, refuge, and salvation. Forgive us for the sins that we commit before you. We know that we are not perfect and make mistakes, so we ask that you continue to use and cover us, helping us to never complain about what comes our way or what we may have to do to help another.

We know that we are not alone, and that prayer is powerful. Through our phones and our social media, we can pray together…even when we are physically far apart, we are still spiritually connected. Now Lord, you can pray with us continually as we are together every day. You tell us that when two or three are gathered in your name, you are in their midst. Thank you, Abba. We love you; we appreciate you, we adore you. Father, we seek your heart for our hurting world.

> *"O Lord, you are my God;*
> *I will exalt you and praise your name, for in perfect faithfulness*
> *you have done marvelous things, things planned long ago."*
> **(Isaiah 25:1 NIV)**

We praise you, Lord, because you complete your plans as promised, in *your* timing, not ours. I pray that we will be patient and still because you are in control no matter what comes our way. Thank you, Father God, for who you are. Let us praise you for the answered prayers, let us praise you for your goodness and your faithfulness, in Jesus' mighty name.

> *"Ask and it will be given to you; seek and you will find; knock and the door will be opened to you. For everyone who asks receives; the one who seeks finds; and to the one who knocks, the door will be opened."*
> **(Matthew 7:7-8 NIV)**

Lord, I pray that we remember that whatever we pray for you will bring to pass. You are a God that will not lie because your Word does not come back void.

> *"So is my word that goes out from my mouth: it will not return to me empty but will accomplish what I desire and achieve the purpose for which I sent it."*
> **(Isaiah 55:11 NIV)**

Thank you, Lord, for your words. I pray that as we are praying together daily during such a time as this, that this too shall come to pass, in Jesus' mighty name. As we pray, we must be careful not to try and fit you into our mold, but instead to make our plans and purposes conform to yours; to honor you, and give you glory in Jesus' name. Everything happens in your time, not ours.

> **GOD WILL HONOR THE DESIRE OF OUR HEARTS...DO NOT FORGET THAT. HE KNOWS WHAT IS BEST FOR US AND WILL BRING IT ABOUT IN DUE TIME.**

We thank you, Lord God, for you are amazing. You are worthy and faithful. I declare that the movement, power, and anointing of God is moving throughout this world, in the name of Jesus Christ, our Lord and Savior, who died for our sins. Thank you, Abba. We praise you. We glorify you. We magnify you. We worship you. We thank you for who you are.

Father God, we know that some are not okay, some are drained, working hard, or are losing their minds trying to help others. I lift up those who are dealing with this, in the name of Jesus. I ask that you calm their minds, heal their hearts, and take away their worries. They are your children, and they need your help.

There are many who are struggling mentally and emotionally. We come against all of that, in the precious wonderful name of Jesus Christ. We cancel every suicidal thought, depression, and anxiety…we rebuke it all, in Jesus' mighty name. We come against the lies and the works of the enemy and cast down the thoughts of those who may be thinking that they will return to their addictions (drugs, alcohol, codependency, eating disorders, compulsive behaviors, or anything that is not good.) We cast it all down, in the name of Jesus. We plead the blood of Jesus Christ over all who are dealing with struggles and challenges.

> *"Therefore, I tell you, do not worry about your life, what you will eat or drink; or about your body, what you will wear. Is not life more important than food, and the body more important than clothes? Look at birds of the air; they do not sow or reap or store away in barns; and yet your Heavenly Father feeds them. Are you not much more valuable than they? Who of you by worrying can add a single hour to his life?"*
> ***(Matthew 6:25-27 NIV)***

## GOD DOES NOT IGNORE THOSE WHO DEPEND ON HIM.

Lord, I come against worry because it shows a lack of faith. I pray that we will live one day at a time, knowing that this can keep us from being consumed with worry. Father God, remind us that when we wake up in the morning, we must seek you first in prayer, putting on the full armor of God…

- The helmet of salvation
- The breastplate of righteousness
- The shield of faith
- The belt of truth
- The gospel of peace for our feet
- The sword of the spirit…your Word

*"Consider it pure joy, my brothers and sisters, whenever you face trials of many kinds, because you know that the testing of your faith produces perseverance. Let perseverance finish its work so that you may be mature and complete, not lacking anything."*
***(James 1:2-4 NIV)***

# Day 16
## THANK HIM FOR HIS PRESENCE

*Heavenly Father*, this is the day you have made. Let us rejoice, both taking joy from it and being so joyful that it rubs off on others. Thank you for waking us up and breathing air into our lungs again. We are alive and that is a blessing. We have a pulse because of you. Thank you, Abba. We love you and appreciate you. You are not finished with us yet.

Lord, all we want is you, all we need is you. As we cry out to you this morning, you know us, and you know what is best for your children. Father God, we are right here, seeking after you. We are *hungry…thirsty…desperate* for you. We cannot live one day without your presence…every encounter changes us when we are with you in your presence, Abba.

I pray that we will cast all our cares and worries on you, surrendering all to you and withholding nothing. Take the weight off of us right now, in the mighty name of Jesus. Lord, thank you that prayer is designed to help us have honest conversations with you in such a time as this…a time when we are all searching for answers. I pray that we turn our hearts and minds toward you and your kingdom.

Jesus, no matter what is going on, let us lift our hands right now, this morning, praising you today, because you are our Redeemer, our Lord, our Savior, our Provider…the One who fights for us, the One who intercedes for us, the One who died to give us life! We love you, Son of God. Thank you for cleansing and forgiving us. Help us to continue to enjoy greater love, peace, joy, and strength. We are sons and daughters of you, our loving Heavenly Father.

Jesus, you are the way to lasting happiness and salvation.

> *"For God so loved the world that He gave His one and only Son, that whoever believes in Him shall not perish but have eternal life."*
> ***(John 3:16 NIV)***

You are amazing, worthy, and faithful. Thank you, Abba, for setting the pattern of true love. You paid dearly with the life of your Son; the highest price Jesus could pay for us! Thank you, Jesus, for accepting our punishment; paying the price for our sins and offering us the new life that you bought for us. I pray that when we share the gospel with others, our love would be like that of Jesus; willingly giving up our own comfort and security so that others might join us in receiving God's love. Especially in such a time because this trying time is a perfect opportunity for everyone to be born again, accepting Christ into their life. Hallelujah! Thank you, Abba for your Son Jesus Christ.

Lord, I pray that we continue to serve, obey, love and do whatever you call us to do, in Jesus' name. I pray that we remember that Jesus' sacrifice is allowing us to find meaning in life and grow to our full potential. We can live a good life when we are following Jesus' teachings. We are here to live with you and our families. We are here to enjoy life no matter what comes our way because you go before us. Lord, thank you that we can cry out to you.

> *"During the days of Jesus' life on earth, He offered up prayers and petitions with loud cries and tears to the one who could save him from death, and he was heard because of his reverent submission."*
> ***(Hebrews 5:7 NIV)***

If you have ever felt that God didn't hear your prayers, remember that we are to pray with reverent submission, respecting Him and being willing to do what He wants. Lord you respond to your obedient children. Thank you, Abba, for drawing near to us, your children. We need you because we know that you are always in control. I pray that in such a time as this, we remain in obedience because we know you can help us obey…no matter how difficult it seems to be.

> **GOD'S PROTECTION IS LIMITLESS.
> ALL WE HAVE TO DO IS LOOK TO HIM,
> FOR HE IS OUR PLACE OF SAFETY WHERE
> THE ENEMY CANNOT FOLLOW. HIS SHIELD
> COMES BETWEEN US AND HARM.**

I pray that we would put our trust in you, remembering that you are with us and not worrying or doubting anything. We thank you; we magnify you; we pray all, in Jesus' name. Amen.

> *"I love you, Lord, my strength. The Lord is my rock, my fortress and my deliverer; my God is my rock, in whom I take refuge, my shield and the horn of my salvation, my stronghold."*
> **(Psalm 18:1-2 NIV)**

# Day 17
## Praise Him for Being Our Refuge

*F*ather in Heaven, King of Glory…we adore your name and work to glorify you forever. Your name is glorious and wonderful, for you are gracious. Thank you for such a wonderful morning. You woke us up even as others did not wake, and we know you are not finished with us yet. Thank you for never leaving our side. We deserve nothing, but you give us everything. Thank you for being there to help, providing refuge, security, and peace. Lord, your power is complete, and your ultimate victory is certain. You will not fail to rescue those who love you, and we are a living witness. A miracle. A true testimony.

> *"Led in with joy and gladness; they enter the palace of the king."*
> ***(Psalm 45:15 NIV)***

Thank you, Jesus. Thank you that all the nations of the earth will eventually recognize your Lordship, because you are powerful, real, and unstoppable… the King of Kings and the Lord of Lords.

> *"The Lord Almighty is with us;*
> *the God of Jacob is our fortress.*
> *Come and see what the Lord has done,*
> *the desolations he has brought on the earth.*
> *He makes wars cease to the ends of the earth.*
> *He breaks the bow and shatters the spear;*
> *he burns the shields with fire.*

*He says, 'Be still, and know that I am God;
I will be exalted among the nations,
I will be exalted in the earth.'
The Lord Almighty is with us;
the God of Jacob is our fortress."*
**(Psalm 46:7-11 NIV)**

We just have to thank the Lord Almighty for being with us during such a time as this. Knowing that He is still in control is such an amazing feeling to have inside. We do not have to doubt if He is with us because His Word tells us that the Lord Almighty is with us and is our fortress.

Thank you, Abba, for being so faithful and worthy. Thank you for such a time as this, because right now it is proper for us to be still, honoring you and your power and majesty. We pray…we *declare* in the precious wonderful name of Jesus that we will take time each day to be still and exalt you Abba; we give you the honor and glory. Thank you for your only Son. We love you Lord, and we magnify you.

*"Jesus said, 'Father, forgive them, for they do not know what they
are doing.' And they divided up His clothes by casting lots."*
**(Luke 23:34 NIV)**

Father, you are so gracious; you thought of us and sent your Son Jesus. He carried His cross to die for us…that is how much we are loved. Lord, teach us how to leave ourselves behind as we shoulder that cross and follow you, remembering that in you, our loss is really a gain. Hallelujah! Abba, thank you for the life in you. Thank you for being our shield and protector.

*"Praise be to the Lord, to God our Savior, who daily bears our burdens."*
**(Psalm 68:19 NIV)**

I declare that we cast off whatever is weighing us down…that we give it to you, in Jesus' name. I pray that we let no problem overtake us. That we do not grow tired or weak, because you give us strength. We know that we can't always control how we respond, but I declare that we will have a desire to seek you first thing in the morning no matter what comes our way. You are in control, so we shall not worry, but walk by faith and not by sight, putting our full trust in you, Abba. I pray that we remember to give thanks to you for the good in our life, and that the parts that seem bad start to seem less significant.

I declare that we will choose to keep a positive attitude and a thankful heart at such a time as this regardless of what we may be going through, and that we rest in the promise that at the right time and with perfect justice, God shall arise.

Thank you, Abba, that we have received righteousness through your Son Jesus Christ. You are going to give us the strength we need to get through this, and we have to trust in that. I declare that we trust in you, and that you will continue to move us forward in such a time as this. Abba, I pray that we remain still and patient, knowing that we will hear you. We will stand firm in our faith, get into your Word even more, and stay prayed up, coming into agreement, in Jesus' mighty name.

Thank you, Lord that we do not focus on money, titles, and prestige, because none of those are important. Love, faith, honesty, goodness, endurance, and caring for others are more important and *"the greatest of these is love." (1 Corinthians 13:13 NIV)* Lord, thank you that your truth always protects, always trusts, always hopes and always perseveres. Thank you that love is available to everyone and that you are so worthy and amazing. Help us to keep your Word in our hearts, in Jesus' name.

## Closing Prayer

> *"In the morning, Lord, you hear my voice; in the morning I lay my requests before you and wait expectantly. For you are not a God who is pleased with wickedness; with you, evil people are not welcome. The arrogant cannot stand in your presence. You hate all who do wrong; you destroy those who tell lies. The bloodthirsty and deceitful you, Lord, detest."*
> **(Psalm 5:3-6 NIV)**

*"The name of the Lord is a strong tower. The righteous run to it and are safe."*
***(Proverbs 18:10 NIV)***

Abba, we thank you for who you are, the King of Kings and the Lord of Lords. Father God, we have a wonderful time here in your presence, and we want to thank you for filling this place with joy and peace. As we go about our day, I ask that you be with us; walk with us and talk with us, everywhere we go and whatever we do. Lord, may your angels go before us and clear the way so that every pastor, minister, prophet, evangelist, teacher, worker from home, those still at their workplace, doctors, lawyers, nurses, CNA workers, home caregivers… all essential workers. Help them to keep your Word in their hearts, and fill them with strength, peace, and joy, in Jesus' mighty name. Lord, these workers have been doing an amazing job of taking care of your people, serving and helping when others may have quit. Lord, we plead the blood of Jesus over them, that they are covered and protected, because you are keeping them all safe, in Jesus' mighty name. Thank you for preparing them beforehand. Lord, we know sometimes, we are caught off guard; but you, Almighty God, have always been before us and are even now, right here, in the midst of it all, covering us, because you knew beforehand that Satan was out to kill, steal, and destroy. But God, you are before us and are with us now. I declare that we will not submit to these circumstances but to you who controls these circumstances. For we know we can't do anything except be still, obey the law, be patient, stay prayed up, come in agreement, read your Word, study it, and apply it to our life, in Jesus' name.

I declare that we will stand firm in our faith. We will resist the devil and all the lies and works of the enemy, coming against anything that tries to cripple our lives, finances, marriages, and health. I pray against the spirit of rejection, grief, shame, failure, setback, and drought. I revoke all spells and demonic spirits, and I come against any hatred and jealousy against our life and in our homes. I rebuke every death sentence against our families and our bodies. I overturn all by the blood of Jesus and the power of His name. No weapon formed against us shall prosper! In Jesus' name. Amen.

We are not alone. Be patient, be still, and trust God. The secret of a close relationship with God is to pray to Him earnestly each morning, when our minds are free from problems, and we can commit the whole day to Him!

# Day 18
## THANK HIM FOR HEARING US

Mighty God, Father in Heaven…thank you that you hear and answer our prayers. Lord, hear our prayer and be in the midst of us today, in Jesus' name. Your Word says that when two or three are gathered in your name, you are in the midst. Thank you that your presence calms the troubled sea of life and speaks peace to our souls. Father give us clear minds and peaceful hearts as we gather together, still spiritually connected, in Jesus' mighty name. We thank you for your Son Jesus Christ, the Savior of the world.

Jesus, we want to thank you for feeling the pain, guilt, and suffering that we experience as a consequence of wrong choices. Thank you for paying the price for our wrongdoings on earth. I declare that repentance and acceptance of your commandments and divine role as our Redeemer shall take place in everyone's lives. Thank you, Jesus, for knowing each of us. I declare that everyone will start to reach out to you so that they can start to know you too.

> *"For everyone born of God overcomes the world. This is the victory that has overcome the world, even our faith. Who is it that overcomes the world? Only he who believes that Jesus is the Son of God."*
> **(1 John 5:4-5 NIV)**

Abba, we thank you for Jesus. We know that our walk is not easy, and that we need you. When life gets hard and serving you is difficult, I pray that we trust in you, knowing that you help us when our load starts to feel heavy.

> *"We know also that the Son of God has come and has given us understanding, so that we may know Him who is true. And we are in Him who is true, even in His Son Jesus Christ. He is the true God and eternal life."*
> **(1 John 5:20 NIV)**

Thank You, Abba. You are amazing, and we glorify and appreciate you. If you had not sent your Son Jesus, we would not be here. We give you the glory Lord God, our Heavenly Father.

> *"Do not be anxious about anything, but in every situation, by prayer and petition, with thanksgiving, present your requests to God."*
> **(Philippians 4:6 NIV)**

I pray that we will cast all our cares and worries to you this day. Lord, replace them with your perfect peace. I declare that we are confident you will do so, in Jesus' name. Thank you for loving us; for forgiving us and healing us, your children. Family, we are beautifully, wonderfully, and uniquely created by God. We praise and honor you, Abba. Help us in such a time as this to keep our eyes fixed on you.

We pray for those who are financially hurting. Lord, you know what we are going through, and we know that you can take the hardest circumstances and turn them around for our good and your glory. Thank you, Lord, that you can restore *all* things. We ask you, in Jesus' name, to restore our lost jobs, finances, relationships, resources, and hope. Lord, for those who are struggling financially, I ask that you show them that you hold them close and that you are surrounding them during their struggle. Please meet their immediate needs as they trust you for long term solutions.

> *"And my God will meet all your needs according to the riches of His glory."*
> **(Philippians 4:19 NIV)**

Thank you for your truth and for your promises to your children. We declare that our fear will turn to faith, in Jesus' name. You are good all the time, and your good plans will unfold, in Jesus' mighty name. Show them Lord; remind them that they are your children of value. Renew their hope, and fill them with courage and peace to move forward. Lord, only you can do it.

Thank you for your promises, Abba. We trust in you, for your Word is our powerful weapon. I declare that we will use your Word every day, keeping it in our hearts. God, you are our Father and our boss. When we remain connected as ambassadors of Christ, our prayers become more powerful.

Thank you, Abba. We are so grateful for you and we praise you.

Lord, we thank you for such a time as this, that you are in the midst of it all. Thank you for your blessings and for providing and supplying our needs. Lord, we lift up our pastors before you; we pray that all is going well in their lives. They are human just like we are, Lord. Fill them with strength, peace, and joy, and remind them that it is okay to relax, take their time, and not rush anything. Ease their minds Abba. I pray healing over them. If at any time they are not well, overturn all by the blood of Jesus and by the power of His name. No weapon formed against them shall prosper, and I rebuke every lie and work of the enemy that tries to come near them. I cast down every lie and declare that our pastors will continue to grow and move forward, in Jesus' name. Thank you, Lord, for who you are and for choosing such amazing, wonderful pastors to lead and help your people. You are worthy and faithful, Lord. Have your way, Abba, have your way. You are still in control, and I pray that we stay humble, patient, still, committed, and faithful to you, knowing that everything is all in your timing, not ours. In Jesus' name. Amen.

# Day 19
## THANK HIM FOR THE LAMB

Mighty God, we thank you for who you are, Prince of Peace. We honor you and magnify you. We thank you for your Son. In the name of Jesus Christ, I come into agreement, remembering that when two or three are gathered in your name, you are in their midst. Thank you for your promises. We appreciate you, and we are so grateful for you. Thank you for your Son, who is the Lamb that takes away the sins of the world. You created this world, and you are still in control.

You are a merciful God who hears the prayers of anyone who calls upon your name with a humble heart and contrite spirit. Lord you hold the stars in the palm of your hand, and you care and love everyone from every nation, race, and tribe. We place our trust in your hands today. Your Word says that *"no weapon formed against us shall prosper"* **(Isaiah 54:17 NIV)**. Therefore, we have nothing to fear…and that includes what's going today. You tell us that you have not given us the spirit of fear, but one of love, power, and of a sound mind, and so we will not be afraid of any sickness or terror. Lord, let us walk fearlessly through this life, knowing that no matter what comes our way, you will always have our back.

Lord, we know that we have the power of your Holy Spirit living within us. We will rely on your sovereign protection because you promised that we should not fear the terror at night or the arrow that flies by day. Abba, we plead for protection against any single thing that roams around us that is not of you. Send your warring angels to defend and protect your people as we put our trust in you.

Abba, we thank you for being so faithful and worthy. You are amazing and so gracious. We know that nothing in this world is able to stand against you. The devil may try to attack us with everything that he has, but when we put on the full armor of God: the helmet of salvation, the breastplate of righteousness, the shield of faith, the belt of truth, the sword of the spirit, and the gospel of peace, nothing can touch us. When we walk by faith and not by sight, you promise us that you will fight our battles. You will make a way when we don't see a way.

You are a miracle worker and a promise keeper and so much more. Father, help us to stay rooted in your Word, because we know times such as this will come; tough, hard, rough challenges that may leave us with heavy hearts, drained with worries of life, stress, and distractions of this world, and feeling our body growing weak from the work we do. We will have moments of exhaustion, and it is okay when we feel drained, because working this hard is not easy. Jesus was drained because He was always teaching, preaching, ministering, and healing out of His overflow. He had to withdraw and have His private time with His Father. We need to recharge, pray, fast, and spend time with our Heavenly Father just like Jesus did.

It is okay to not have it all figured out, because you already do. I declare that we will never give up, starting and ending our day with prayer.

> **WHEN PRAYER BECOMES OUR HABIT, MIRACLES BECOME OUR LIFESTYLE.**

When facing overwhelming circumstances, we put them into your hands and say, *"God's got this!"* We will never walk alone, because we have Jesus. Thank you, Abba, for being with us. We love you and adore you. Father God, I declare that peace will prevail on earth, in Jesus' mighty name.

> *"Rejoice in the Lord always. I will say it again. Rejoice! Let your gentleness be evident to all. The Lord is near. Do not be anxious about anything but in everything, by prayer and petition, with thanksgiving, present your requests to God. And the peace of God, which transcends all understanding, will guard your hearts and your minds in Christ Jesus."*
> **(Philippians 4:4-7 NIV)**

As a child of God, you are…

Healed…*Favored*…Restored…*Blessed*…Unique…
*Special*…Lovely…*Precious*…Strong…*Chosen*.

No matter what is happening in your life, *do not* forget who you are in God.

# Day 20
## THANK HIM FOR HIS FAVOR

Almighty God, we come before you in the precious wonderful name of Jesus Christ. Father, forgive us for our sins. Thank you for waking us up this very morning, and for breathing in us again.

Thank you for your grace; we praise you in the house of the Lord. All of our homes are your house, Father. We have gathered to thank you; to glorify, honor, and appreciate you. You are so gracious…you have kept us alive to praise and worship your Holy Name. Your presence brings strength, peace, and hope into our lives. Thank you, Lord God, for washing us clean through your mercy. Abba, we thank you for your *presence*…your *protection*…your *safety*…and your *covering* over us. We know that we are all still spiritually connected no matter what is going on. We still have unity in the Body of Christ.

> *"Now to him who is able to do immeasurably more than all we ask or imagine, according to his power that is at work within us, to him be glory in the church and in Christ Jesus throughout all generations, for ever and ever! Amen."*
> **(Ephesians 3:20-21 NIV)**

Thank you for your truth, Lord. I declare that we will proclaim your truth with a sincere heart. I declare that we keep our Bibles—your instructions to us, your Word—close to our hearts, so that we would obey and be successful, in Jesus' mighty name. Jesus came for a mission, and now it is ours to announce the truth to the whole world: that God is real, powerful, and unstoppable. He is the King of Kings and the Lord of Lords. I declare we will abide in the Word.

We will know the Truth, and we will be set free indeed. Lord, help us to spend time in your Word so that we will continue to grow in our understanding of you and your ways. I declare that we will learn how to pattern our lives after the truth we have read and that we will keep your Word on our lips and meditate on it day and night.

> *"Make every effort to keep the unity of the Spirit through the bond of peace. There is one body and one Spirit, just as you were called to one hope when you were called; one Lord, one faith, one baptism; one God and Father of all, who is over all and through all and in all."*
> ***(Ephesians 4:3-6 NIV)***

Hallelujah! Thank you, Lord, for being over all of us. Thank you for your overruling care that shows your active presence in the world and the lives of believers. Lord, we thank you for who you are, and we love you. You love us so much, and I pray that we remember that all believers in Christ belong to one body; we are united under one head, Christ Himself. As believers, we have God-given abilities that can strengthen the whole body. Lord, we know that often, we may be separated because of minor differences in doctrine; but we are a spiritual family of believers that we will attain true unity, in Jesus' name. I declare that through this unity of spirit, we will never allow difficult circumstances to separate us, because we are all one body, one spirit, one hope, one Lord, one faith, one baptism, and one God, who keeps us for eternity. Thank You, Jesus.

Father God, you are so faithful. You never promised that there would be no distractions, disappointments, challenges, difficult circumstances, or pain. You never promised things would always be easy and that we would never be afraid. But Almighty Heavenly Father, you *did* promise that you would be faithful in every season and keep us strong.

> *"He will also keep you strong to the end, so that you will be blameless on the day of our Lord Jesus Christ. God is faithful, who has called you into fellowship with his Son Jesus Christ our Lord."*
> ***(1 Corinthians 1:8-9 NIV)***

All who believe in the Lord Jesus will be considered blameless. I pray that during a time such as this, that the whole world will search for you in the midst of the bad. Thank you, Lord, that during these difficult times, we have witnessed you moving in amazing ways. Thank you for this spiritual awakening; that we are still moving forward and that your Word and your truth are still covering the whole world. It is amazing to see people searching for answers and hope, finding an invitation into a relationship with God. They are turning to the author and finisher of it all. Hallelujah! We thank you Lord for being in our midst, in Jesus' name. Amen.

## Closing Prayer

Thank you for your Son who died on the cross for our sins, for the gift of creation, and for allowing us to see another day. All honor, glory, and praise be to your name. We love you in the name of Jesus Christ.

God is right with us. He knew what would be going on today. He still has a plan, because He is still in control and in charge. He's got the whole world in His hands and we have nothing to fear. We stand firm in faith. I pray that we will be still and remain humble, trusting in God and walking by faith. In Jesus' name. Amen.

We are favored and blessed.

We are…

- Not alone.
- In this together.
- Children of God.
- His sons and daughters…and He is with us, providing and supplying all our needs.

**FAITH OVER FEAR**

# Day 21
## PRAISE HIM FOR BEING OUR DWELLING PLACE

Heavenly Father…King of Glory…we adore your wonderful name and work to glorify you forever. We come before you, in the name of your Son Jesus, and we thank you for breathing in us again this very morning, for we know others across this earth did not wake up. We thank you for waking us up, Heavenly Father. You are our gracious provider, maker, and protector.

> *"The Lord is my light and my salvation—whom shall I fear? The Lord is the stronghold of my life—of whom shall I be afraid?"*
> ***(Psalm 27:1 NIV)***

Thank you, Abba, that when we dwell in your presence, we have nothing to worry about; we are in good standing with you. Thank you for your shadow that covers us. I declare that we will dwell in the house of the Lord all the days of our lives, in Jesus' mighty name. I declare that we will gaze upon the beauty of the Lord and seek you morning, noon, and night, in Jesus' name.

> *"For in the day of trouble he will keep me safe in his dwelling; he will hide me in the shelter of his sacred tent and set me high upon a rock. Then my head will be exalted above the enemies who surround me; at his sacred tent I will sacrifice with shouts of joy; I will sing and make music to the Lord."*
> ***(Psalm 27:5-6 NIV)***

> # HALLELUJAH! WE MAY HAVE **DONE** WHAT THE DEVIL SAID WE **DID**, BUT WE ARE **NOT** WHO THE DEVIL SAYS WE **ARE**!

We are children of the Most High God; the King of Kings and the Lord of Lords. Our Father loved us so much that we are called children of God, and we really are His children, because we know Him. When we have been seeking Him and serving Him with a sincere and true heart, we know who He is in our lives. Thank you, Jesus. Lord we know many may fail because they are afraid to try. Lord we come against the lies and works of the enemy and declare that all of your children will start seeking you, getting to know who you are by reading your Word. I declare that this whole world will receive a Bible and that they will be transformed by applying your truth to their life, in Jesus' mighty name.

We have the perfect opportunity during such a time as this. Abba, I pray that we all will be like Christ, for He is pure, and all who have this hope in Him will keep themselves pure like Him. When we trust in God, we will never be put to shame or disappointed. At such a time as this, help us not to worry if anyone puts us down. I declare that we will continue to speak your great Word; your message of truth and salvation to others so that they can respond to the Good News. Lord, thank you for such a time as this because your Word is now across this whole world, where everyone can see and hear it. Amazing it is, indeed.

You are changing and transforming this world to see you, Abba. When people complain that they can't make it to church or that we need prayer, there are no more excuses because you are alive. The world would come to know you Lord…I speak it. We have victory and a new life in Jesus.

Thank you, Abba. We love and adore you. What the enemy meant for evil, you have turned around for your good. Thank you for your faithfulness. You are so worthy and good. Family, we are God's gift, and we are becoming a gift to God. We want Him to change our situation, but He wants to change us. Everything may not be perfect. There are things that may need to change…but we have the grace to be happy today. We awoke with joy because we are blessed from

God. We have directed our prayers unto Him, and we have looked up to our Heavenly Father, in Jesus' name.

Abba, we thank you for helping us and drawing near to us. Thank you for being in the midst of it all. We ask that you protect and cover us. Keep us safe; preserve and bless us. Reach each person in our family, in our circle of friends, and across this world, in Jesus' mighty name. Lord, I pray that we never again take for granted birthdays, family days, sitting with children, smiling, laughing with one another, visiting loved ones at home or in a hospital, health, gatherings, coffee with others, hugs, kisses, love…I pray that we appreciate that we are still here and breathing. We have to praise and thank God for taking care of us and keeping us spiritually connected. He has been so amazing and wonderful.

Prayer has been letting us know what you have been doing. We know that many have passed. You have called many of our friends and family home, and I pray that we will remember that when we walk through the valley, we have peace; and that in some situations, our prayer may be the very instrument God plans to use in bringing about the result He desires. God wants to involve us in His work; and that includes our prayers. Have your way Lord, in Jesus' name. Amen.

# Day 22
## THANK HIM FOR HIS TRANSFORMING LOVE

Heavenly Father, we come before you in the precious name of your Son Jesus.

> *"Truly I tell you, whatever you bind on earth will be bound in heaven, and whatever you loose on earth will be loosed in heaven. Again, truly I tell you that if two of you on earth agree about anything they ask for, it will be done for them by my Father in heaven. For where two or three are gathered in my name, there am I with them."*
> *(Matthew 18:18-20 NIV)*

Hallelujah. Thank you, Abba, that you are in the midst of us. Thank you for waking us up this morning. We are blessed. You love us, and you are not finished with us yet. Thank you that we can come to you for guidance in seeking you to resolve conflict. Hallelujah. Thank you, Jesus. We praise you; we give you the glory and thank you for who you are.

Thank you, Lord God, for being in the midst of our prayers and our lives. Thank you that you are present with us, not in body but through your Holy Spirit. We are here today to pray according to your will, not our own, making our requests in Jesus' mighty name.

Lord, quiet our minds and still our hearts, for your living ways are all we seek. Strengthen our lives. Inspire our spirits, in Jesus' mighty name. We have been starting our days together in agreement with prayer and praise, which I believe leads us to peace and provision from you to make it through the day.

## WE DO NOT KNOW WHAT **TODAY HOLDS**… BUT WE KNOW WHO **HOLDS TODAY**!

> *"'I am the Alpha and the Omega,' says the Lord God, 'who is, and who was, and who is to come, the Almighty.'"*
> **(Revelation 1:8 NIV)**

Hallelujah. Thank you, Abba, for being the beginning and the end. God you are our eternal Lord and ruler of the past, present, and future. Without you, we are nothing. We have nothing. We need you because you are eternal and as believers, we need to accept Christ in our lives and live with Him and for Him, because without Him there is no transformation.

Thank you for your forgiveness. Lord, I pray that we know that Jesus is the reason for all seasons; because without Him, none of us would have been saved from our own sinful nature. Lord, you are our reason for living…the Alpha and Omega of our lives. We honor you, Lord. You are the beginning and ending of all existence, wisdom, and power.

Hallelujah! We praise you. You are amazing and so gracious, Abba. You are still in control, no matter the circumstances. You are powerful and unstoppable, and we glorify you and give you all the glory. You have been so good to us.

Thank you, Jesus. There is a song of joy and victory that we have been walking in your power, and it has been within us, in Jesus' name.

Abba, with all that has been going on in these stressful times, there has been an invitation to enter joyfully into your presence. Because we are still here and breathing, you are not finished yet. Hallelujah! You have been victorious over the evil that has tried to hinder us. We praise you, Abba. Thank you for your faithfulness…you are so worthy. We praise you for your fairness and holiness. We trust you completely, for you are good all the time. You are so good, and I declare that we will shout for joy, giving you the glory because we are still here and no weapon formed against us shall prosper. In Jesus' mighty name. Hallelujah.

> *"Shout for joy to the Lord, all the earth. Worship the Lord with gladness; come before him with joyful songs. Know that the Lord is God. It is he who made us, and we are his; we are his people, the sheep of his pasture. Enter his gates with thanksgiving and his courts with praise; give thanks to him and praise his name. For the Lord is good and his love endures forever; his faithfulness continues through all generations."*
> **(Psalm 100:1-5 NIV)**

Hallelujah!

God is our Creator and we do not have to worry about anything because He is still in control, no matter what we see. At first, we may think, *"Why us, God?"* Trying to resist Him may have worked for a while, but we have all seen how good God is, our Father, our Abba. We gave in, finding out that giving in and accepting Christ was infinitely better than our old life before. We have been blown away. Hallelujah! Thank you, Jesus!

> ENCOUNTERING JESUS HAS BEEN A RADICAL EXPERIENCE, AND IT DEMANDS FROM US A RADICAL RESPONSE. HALLELUJAH!

We have victory in Christ; we are new creations, the old has gone. I declare that we will not look back at our old habits, because we are free indeed. Thank you, Jesus. You are so worthy and faithful. You made a way, in Jesus' name. Amen.

# Closing Prayer

Lord, we want to thank you for this spiritual connection, full of joy and peace, in Jesus' name.

> *"This is the day which the Lord hath made;*
> *we will rejoice and be glad in it."*
> **(Psalm 118:24 KJV)**

Rejoice in the Lord always. I say it again. *Rejoice!* I declare that our hearts will be filled with your amazing words and promises, in Jesus' name. Lord, we come against the lies and the works of the enemy. We plead the blood of Jesus by the power of His mighty name.

Thank you, Almighty God, for the strongholds that you are removing in such a time as this. What the enemy has intended for evil, you have seen for your good. God bless us, your children, with true wisdom and good health. Your goodness and mercy shall follow us all the days of our life, in Jesus' mighty name. I decree and declare that miracles happen when you move; this is a move you have been waiting for, Lord. Miracles, signs, and wonders. Thank you, Abba, for the revivals, testimonials, reconnections, restarting, and so much more that you are doing. We are at a turning point, and we will not fear. We are humble before you because when we get you, we get everything we need. Every encounter has been changing us, in Jesus' name; I declare and decree that it is so.

We are not alone. We are spiritually connected and unified with God by our sides. Stay encouraged, and do not worry or fear. Remember to have faith over fear. We put on the full armor of God, in Jesus' mighty name. Amen.

# Day 23
# Thank Him for Humility and Grace

Heavenly Father, we thank you. We give you praise and honor, and we glorify you because of who you are. You are a present help in our time of need. I pray that we do not let yesterday take up too much of today. Have your way in our life, and do what you want to do, in Jesus' name. This is a new day; a fresh day. Thank you for breathing in us, Abba, for you are not finished with us yet. I pray that we devote whatever you have entrusted us with to doing good…all possible good…in every possible kind and degree…in Jesus' mighty name.

Lord, we know that when you are our best friend, we are never alone. I declare that we will never quit praying, for we know that you can do anything in our lives instantly. We believe in you, Lord God. You have been showing us during this time that we are in—a season of humbling ourselves and surrendering to your plan. You have been saying, *"Be humble,"* just as Jesus did when He preached, for He was an expert in humility. Jesus traded a kingly crown for a thorny one, for our sake.

> *"When someone invites you to a wedding feast, do not take the place of honor, for a person more distinguished than you may have been invited. If so, the host who invited both of you will come and say to you, 'Give this person your seat.' Then, humiliated, you will have to take the least important place. But when you are invited, take the lowest place, so that when your host comes, he will say to you, 'Friend, move up to a better place.'*

*Then you will be honored in the presence of all the other guests. For all those who exalt themselves will be humbled, and those who humble themselves will be exalted."*
**(Luke 14:8-11 NIV)**

Lord, when we put you first, I declare that we will remember that everything else will fall into its proper place. We were created to shine; an eternal glory that does not fade, with the help of your Son Jesus, who died for our sins.

We know that when we accept Christ and start to walk with Him, we will have eternal life. Abba, we know in these stressful times it has been heavy, hard, and sad. Many have lost their loved ones and have not been well even though they are believing for healing and to be able to see their families. Lord, we ask for grace, mercy, and blessings to take place, in Jesus' mighty name. We believe in the power of prayer.

Jesus, touch the people around us. Keep them safe; protect them, comfort them, heal the sick, and protect those that are not; give them love, compassion, and care. Bless them with good health and peace of mind. Keep them joyful no matter what is going on, because you still are in control and will always have the final say. Cover us with your precious and holy blood, as well as our family, friends, and life projects. Abba, give us your dream. Bless and protect everyone who seeks you, needs you, and believes in you in Jesus' name.

We thank you, Father God, for loving us and drawing near to us. Thank you for who you are; for hearing our cries, our screams, our shouts, and our mourning. Thank you for wrapping your arms around us when you know we need your touch. Thank you, Abba, that we are your sons and daughters. I pray that we will trust in you, walking by faith and not by sight. We will be patient and still, not fearing anything because you knew everything before we all were formed in the womb.

You knew two thousand years ago what our lives would be like. Everything is in your control and under your timing, not ours. As we humble ourselves, I pray that we would move forward by praying, persevering, and prevailing. Breathe on us, Lord. Send your Spirit, in Jesus' mighty name. Abba, just as

Jesus was exalted and now sits on His throne in Heaven, we could all use a lesson in humility from the expert.

Lord, this time has been a blessing. Many have fallen to their knees worshiping you, praising you, and asking for your forgiveness. Rushing things in life has slowed down for the best. Thank you, Abba, for protecting us and thinking of us two thousand years ago. Thank you, Jesus. We love and appreciate you. Thank you, Abba, for slowing our lives to help us become better men and women of God. You deserve all the glory. You are gracious and so mighty.

Thank you for a season of tests. I pray that during these tests, we truly humble and compare ourselves only with Christ, realizing our sinfulness and understanding our limitations. During this time Lord God, may we recognize our gifts and strengths and use them as Christ directs us to. Thank you that humility is not self-degradation; it is a realistic assessment and commitment to serve. It is time to take a leap of faith and trust you. When you step in, the enemy is mad, because he has to stop.

As we learn how to humble ourselves, we can rest assured that we too will be exalted like Jesus! Hallelujah! Abba, you are our help—it all comes from you! It is all on your shoulders. You're lifting us up and we don't have to see it to believe it. Your mercy is relentless. You're right here, pulling us through, spiritually connected as we are, in Jesus' mighty name.

I declare that we will focus and keep our eyes fixed on Jesus, because He will make sure that we are okay. Lord, we ask that you guide the people that make the decisions for our country. We come against harmful decisions, and we cast them down, in Jesus' mighty name. We are believing for greater things, and there will be glory.

# Day 24
## THANK HIM FOR THE GIFT OF OBEDIENCE

Our Father and our God, we bless your name forever. You are worthy of all of our praises, and we thank you for the gift of your Word. We love you, Abba. We glorify and appreciate you. Thank you for the blessings that you have given us and for waking us up this very morning and breathing in us. Thank you for our families, loved ones, and friends. Lord, give us a wonderful morning as we connect, coming into agreement and seeking you because we need you. Thank you that we make room for you. Please live in us, in Jesus' mighty name.

Guide us as we pray. Remove what is in your way, because we don't want it there. I pray that we would withhold nothing and that we would be free from generational curses, bondage, and strongholds, in Jesus' mighty name. I declare that we will have a completely free spiritual walk, truly withholding nothing, giving up control of our life, and trusting in you Abba, because you are still in control and in charge no matter what is going on.

You make all the true and blessed, safe decisions of this nation, in Jesus' name. We will not worry or doubt, because we trust in you. You are working around the clock for us. Hallelujah! You never sleep, Abba. You are so faithful, amazing, worthy, and gracious. You are the beginning and the end, and you own everything. We love you and appreciate you. I pray that we would leave everything in God's hands because we will eventually see His plan—His hand in everything. We cannot let what is going on destroy our inner peace.

> *"And the peace of God, which transcends all understanding, will guard your hearts and your minds in Christ Jesus."*
> **(Philippians 4:7 NIV)**

Pray, then let it go. Trust God to do what He is going to do at the right time.

> *"Therefore, do not worry about tomorrow, for tomorrow will worry about itself. Each day has enough trouble of its own."*
> **(Matthew 6:34 NIV)**

Obey and do what God has told you to do. He will take care of the rest.

> ## "YOU HAVE BEEN ASSIGNED THIS MOUNTAIN TO SHOW OTHERS IT CAN BE MOVED."
> ~MEL ROBBINS

Command and speak to whatever you know you need to let go. Command it to leave your life. Then speak to that which needs to come back into your body or into your life.

God wants us to rise up and use the authority He has given us through Jesus! We have to remember that all God does is good, and His reverence is the beginning of wisdom. He is so amazing. The advantage of having faith in God is that He guards the minds and actions of those who follow His commands. Thank you, Abba, for loving us the way you do. You are so gracious. Thank you for being our light, our salvation and the strength of our life.

Lord God, we have all had our plans disrupted, but you know all, and you know what is best for us. You are still in control. I declare that we will continue to trust in your guidance, because you are the planner who provides and does everything according to your time, not ours. I declare that we will not worry or fear because that would make it difficult to trust you. Thank you, Abba, for slowing everything down…for slowing *us* down, your sons and daughters, because you knew our planning was interfering with our relationship with you.

I declare that we will not let worries about tomorrow affect our relationship with you today. Hallelujah!

> *"'Have faith in God,' Jesus answered. 'Truly I tell you, if anyone says to this mountain, "Go, throw yourself into the sea," and does not doubt in their heart but believes that what they say will happen, it will be done for them. Therefore, I tell you, whatever you ask for in prayer, believe that you have received it, and it will be yours. And when you stand praying, if you hold anything against anyone, forgive them, so that your Father in heaven may forgive you your sins."'*
> **(Mark 11:22-25 NIV)**

Thank you, Lord, for getting our attention in such a time as this. The kind of prayers that move mountains are prayers for the fruitfulness of your Kingdom. During prayer, knowing that we are about to enter your presence, there are always conditions that we must meet. We must be believers, not pray with selfish motives, not hold a grudge against another person, and our request must be for the good of your Kingdom. Lord, as we pray, let our prayers be effective, having faith in you, and not faith in the object of our request. I pray that we will focus not on our request, but on our trust in you. Jesus is our example when He says, *"Everything is possible for you, yet not what I will, but what you will"* **(Luke 22:42 NIV)**. Father God, help us to remember that our prayers are not about our own desires and interests, but our focus on your Son Jesus who prayed with your interests in mind. When we pray, we express our desires, but we want to have your will above ours, in Jesus' name. I pray that our prayers will focus on your interest, in Jesus' mighty name. We know that you are making a way out of every situation. Lord, you saw it all before it came upon this earth and our lives.

> *"Forget the former things;*
> *do not dwell on the past.*
> *See, I am doing a new thing!*
> *Now it springs up; do you not perceive it?*
> *I am making a way in the wilderness*
> *and streams in the wasteland."*
> **(Isaiah 43:18-19 NIV)**

The past miracles were nothing compared to what God would do for His people in the future! God said, *"I need y'all to be patient and wait, trust in me. But I want y'all to strive, to rise up because I am the Way Maker, Miracle Worker, Promise Keeper, Light in the Darkness."* That is who our God is. In Jesus' name. Amen.

# Day 25
## THANK HIM FOR WHAT HE IS YET TO DO

Heavenly Father, our Provider and Protector, we bless your name. We give you all the praise…all the glory…all the honor. You are good all the time. Thank you, Abba. King of Glory, we adore your name and work to glorify you forever, in Jesus' mighty name. Forgive us for our sins that we commit before you.

Lord I pray right now that if there is anyone who has not turned to follow Jesus by living the committed life, that today, they stop their sinful nature and grow tired of seeking their own will and following their own desires, and nail all wrongful doing to the cross, in Jesus' mighty name. Life *without* you is nothing…but life *with* you is eternal. We thank you in advance for what you are going to do. We thank you for who you are. King of Kings and Lord of Lords. Have your way and do what you want to do right now.

You are welcome here, because we know when two or three are gathered in your name, you are in the midst of them. Thank you for your promises and your Word. God thank you for waking us up; we are healthy, we are alive, and we are blessed. You are not finished with us yet, so have your way and do what you do, Abba. We can't control everything. Remind us that sometimes we need to relax and have faith that things will work out. To "let go and let life," because you are in control and in charge. Everything is on your time, not ours. Thank you, Abba, for who you are. We love you. We appreciate you so much. We know that we need you and that we need to breathe, relax, and trust in you. Worrying won't fix it but trusting in you will. I pray that we open our hearts and invite you in…because when you enter the scene, miracles happen. Hallelujah! If anyone is discouraged, right at this very moment, I declare that they fix their eyes on Jesus. In due time, He will restore this old world. Jesus will reign over every inch and every being; and with His reign, there will be justice, blessings, and peace. Lord, reign in our hearts, because we know and believe that you will reign here on earth. Everything belongs to you. You are the glorious eternal King. I pray and declare we worship you and welcome your glorious reign.

> *"The earth is the Lord's and everything in it, the world and all who live in it; For he founded it upon the seas and established it upon the waters."*
> ***(Psalm 24:1-2 NIV)***

Thank You, Abba, for your Word, and for guiding us in the paths of righteousness.

> *"Even though I walk through the valley of the shadow of death, I will fear no evil, for you are with me; your rod and your staff, they comfort me."*
> ***(Psalm 23:4 NIV)***

Thank you, Abba, for walking with us through it all. You are our safety, the God of life, our shepherd. We thank you; for whom shall we fear when we have you near? Hallelujah! When life is uncertain, we have a shepherd that we can and should follow, who offers eternal comfort, in Jesus' name. Hallelujah. Thank you, Daddy God, for your protection when our enemies surround us. You go before us and you are with us.

> *"For the Lord Almighty has purposed, and who can thwart Him? His hand is stretched out and who can turn it back?"*
> ***(Isaiah 14:27 NIV)***

You are real, powerful, and unstoppable. You make miracles happen every second of our lives. When the forces of darkness come, nothing can stop what you have ordained. Thank you that your promises are *"Yes"* and *"Amen."*

Lord, we lift up those battling disease or illness. I declare that every sickness would break up, vanish, and disappear by the power and blood of Jesus' mighty name, for *"nothing is impossible with God." (**Luke 1:37 NIV**)*

Thank You, Abba. You are so amazing and awesome. You get all the glory because it is about *you*, not us. We stand in the gap, coming into agreement and believing and knowing that you are drawing near to us because this is our secret weapon. Whether we pray alone or are spiritually connected, our physical distance means nothing. You are right here in the midst of it all, and we are connected, locking hands with nothing coming between us. Thank you, Abba, for helping us, choosing us, and keeping us alert, with our eyes fixed on Jesus. We know that there is power in prayer and that prayer is a lifetime journey. Prayer is when we are closest to you and reading your Word.

Right now, Lord, I want to lift up our pastors before you. They are ministering to our souls and being a blessing to everyone. They are giving us your Word and your truth. We thank you for they are amazing and awesome, and so faithful and worthy. Thank you for helping them to adjust and adapt so quickly to the changes that you wanted to make in your kingdom. I speak strength, peace, joy, rest, love, relaxation, and goodness over their lives. Supply and provide for all their needs, in Jesus' name. Have your way Lord, have your way. Amen.

## Closing Prayer

Thank you, for your Son, dying on the Cross for our sins, for the gift of your creation, and for allowing us to see another day. All honor, glory, and praise be to your name. Amen.

# Day 26
## Praise Him for Bringing Order Out of Chaos

Almighty Father God, our Protector, our King. Thank you that you woke us up today. We may not know what today will bring, but you, Almighty, know it all. May nothing separate us from you today. Lord, teach us how to choose only your way today so that each step will lead us closer to you, in Jesus' mighty name. Father God, help us to walk by your Word and not our feelings. Help us to keep our hearts pure and undivided.

We know that morning prayer is a wonderful way to focus our time and attention on seeking your plan for the day ahead. Jesus, I ask that you calm the chaos in our spirits. Heavenly Father you are the God of the universe. I pray that we keep asking, seeking, and knocking, and that we remember that a worry list should be a prayer list. Prayer is work; a place to communicate and to listen to you, Lord God. Remind us, Abba, that nothing is more exciting than prayer, and that nothing is supposed to steal our prayer life. I pray that we see things though your eyes and that we all have a "House of Prayer," a place where we listen to you and speak to you.

Thank you that you have the power to change any situation. Thank you that you are working behind the scenes. I pray that we are willing to let go of the old. We thank you Abba, for you are a good Father. We love you; we appreciate you. Thank you for your Son Jesus, and for thinking of us all, your sons and daughters. Thank you that you see order where others see chaos…and that is when you start prioritizing. Keep stirring up a new passion, in Jesus' name.

> *"Lord Almighty, blessed is the one who trusts in you."*
> ***(Psalm 84:12 NIV)***

Help us to embrace what comes our way as an opportunity rather than a personal inconvenience.

> *"Teach me your way, O Lord, and I will walk in your truth; give me an undivided heart, that I may fear your name. I will praise You, O Lord my God, with all my heart; I will glorify your name forever. For great is your love toward me; you have delivered me from the depths of the grave."*
> ***(Psalm 86:11-13 NIV)***

Thank you, Abba, for the great love you have toward us. Thank you for your great and marvelous deeds, *"for you alone are God."* ***(Psalm 86:10 NIV)***

We thank you, Abba, for you are so gracious and our light that shines, no matter what. We know that everything isn't perfect, but we know you are working it out for our good. During times such as this there are blessings that are on the way; but we thank you for the lessons because without them, we cannot grow. Thank you for thinking of us, for loving us the way you do.

Thank you, Abba, for what we have. Even though much is going on in this world, you love us and have been supplying and providing for our needs. Thank you for the food on the table, gas in the cars, those who still have a job, Lord. Hallelujah. You are faithful and worthy. Thank you for keeping every promise you make, in Jesus' name.

> *"Among the gods there is none like you O Lord; no deeds can compare with yours."*
> ***(Psalm 86:8 NIV)***

Abba, that is right…no one is like you. You are the God of the Bible; you are unique, alive, and able to do mighty deeds for those who love you. You alone are worthy, Lord. We will never worship any other gods because you, Abba, are the Lord alone and give us support, love, and forgiveness. You speak to us, you teach us right from wrong, you provide, and you see. Thank you, Abba, for who you are.

You are our peace, our strength, and our salvation. We stand in awe of you… praise be to the Lord Almighty.

> *"Lord, you are my God; I will exalt you and praise your name,*
> *for in perfect faithfulness you have done marvelous things,*
> *things planned long ago."*
> **(Isaiah 25:1 NIV)**

Thank you, Abba, that you complete your plans as promised. I want you to think of an answered prayer and just praise and thank our God for His goodness and faithfulness, because He is so faithful and worthy. Thank You, Jesus! Lord, I pray that we remember that we are children of the Living God, and we have nothing to worry about. You are in control and everything is in your timing. I pray we will be patient, still, humble, committed, and faithful to you, walking by faith, not by sight. We will stand firm in our faith because faith drives out fear. I declare that we will not fear all that is going on, but will cast our cares, anxiety, and worries to you because you love and care for us.

> *"Cast Your burden upon the Lord and He will sustain you;*
> *He will never allow the righteous to be shaken."*
> **(Psalm 55:22 NIV)**

He will never let us fail.

Right now, Abba, we rebuke, cancel, and destroy every assignment and attack of the enemy, and cancel every curse or negative word ever spoken over our life or over this country, in the powerful name of Jesus Christ. Amen.

# Day 27
## THANK HIM FOR HIS FAITHFULNESS

Good morning, Lord! This is the day that you have made, and we will rejoice and be glad in it. We thank you for preserving our life for one more day. With gratitude, we thank you for your ultimate gift of love for us, in the form of your Son and the sacrifice of His life on our behalf. There is much going on, and it is overwhelming; but Lord, teach us your ways that we may rely on your faithfulness. Teach us to trust in you, Lord God. I declare that we will trust in our Almighty Lord God, in Jesus' mighty name.

We do not know what this day holds…but we know that you hold the day. It was you who laid the foundations of the earth and therefore understand every part of it. Father, thank you for keeping the stars in the sky and for creating the earth for us to inhabit and enjoy. I pray that throughout this day, we will be aware of your presence in everything we do, and that our lives will be a living example to those that we come in contact with. May others see Christ in us. Thank You, Abba. Thank you, Jesus. We love you.

> *"Give ear to my words, O Lord, consider my singing. Listen to my cry for help, my King and my God, for to you I pray. In the morning, O Lord, you hear my voice; in the morning I lay my requests before you and wait in expectation. You are not a God who takes pleasure in evil; with you the wicked cannot dwell. The arrogant cannot stand in your presence; you hate all who do wrong. You destroy those who tell lies; bloodthirsty and deceitful men the Lord abhors."*
> ***(Psalm 5:1-6 KJV)***

Thank you, Lord God, that you are able to defend us from lies spoken and decisions that are not made properly. Lord, take over, because we know that you are in control and in charge of the nation. We know that there is deliverance from trouble. We thank you, Almighty God, that you are able to rescue us from the enemy and those who persecute the innocent.

Thank you, Abba, for your faithfulness. We appreciate and magnify you Lord. You are so gracious and good…thank you that we can rejoice in your protection and peace because you are mighty, real, powerful, and unstoppable. I declare that we will place our confidence in you, Lord God, because you will listen when we call on you, in Jesus' name. Hallelujah!

Abba, we know that there are many in this world who are hurting. Lord Jesus, may we be a soothing, healing ointment to your people, in ways that we cannot even imagine. I declare that healing, strength, peace, joy, kindness, love, and the blood of Jesus will cover everyone who is ill. We overturn every sickness right now by the power of Jesus' mighty name. We rebuke, command, and cancel every lie, and destroy every assignment that is an attack of the roaring lion who is roaming around, trying to enter God's children. We cast them down because no weapon formed against His children shall prosper.

I declare and speak healing over God's sons and daughters. We command you devil, in Jesus' mighty name, to take your hands off of His children. They are covered by the blood and powerful name of Jesus Christ.

I declare that our words would be seasoned with salt; keep us salty, Lord, so others will know and notice you. I declare in Jesus' name that we will minister grace to all that hear. That our actions will be aligned with your Word, Daddy God.

Thank you, Abba, for choosing and appointing us. Thank you for loving us so much and always thinking of us, even in such a time as this. Thank you, Jesus. You are our salvation, our light, and our shield of protection. Your Word says, *"for the joy of the Lord is my strength." **(Nehemiah 8:10 NIV)***

Father, I ask that you remove fear and anxiety. As believers you have not given us a spirit of fear, but of love, power, and a sound mind. I pray that we will remember your love for us and that we will tap into the power that you have given us, for we are never alone, because you have not left us comfortless. Help those that worry or fear to turn all of their anxious thoughts and nerve-wracking situations over to you and trust that you are working, in Jesus' mighty name. Remind us that we are fearfully and wonderfully made in your image and that you loved us, your sons and daughters, so much that you thought that we were worth dying for. Lord, we don't know too many people who would die for us, but you did. We are eternally grateful and humbled. Thank you, Jesus.

> *"But let all who take refuge in you be glad; let them ever sing for joy. Spread your protection over them, that those who love your name may rejoice in you. For surely, O Lord, you bless the righteous; you surround them with your favor as with a shield."*
> **(Psalm 5:11-12 NIV)**

Thank you, Abba. You are so good, and we give you all the praise and glory. You deserve it all. I declare that we will confidently trust in you for protection and peace and that we will stand firm in our faith, walking by faith and not by sight, in Jesus' mighty name. Amen.

> *"Be strong and take heart, all you who hope in the Lord."*
> **(Psalm 31:24 NIV)**

---

# THE CLOSER WE WALK WITH GOD, THE LESS ROOM THERE IS FOR ANYTHING TO COME BETWEEN US.

# Day 28
## THANK HIM FOR ANSWERED PRAYERS

Almighty Heavenly Father, we come before you in Jesus' mighty name and by His blood and power, because we need a move. Many have been fasting, waiting, and praying. Have your way, Lord. Move by your spirit because this is a move in Jesus' mighty name. We thank you for being who you are and for being by our side, supplying and providing for our needs. Thank you for answering our prayers for which we been in agreement together and for others we have not heard of yet…but you know and hear them all.

> *"Confess your faults one to another, and pray one for another, that ye may be healed. The effectual fervent prayer of a righteous man availeth much."*
> **(James 5:16 KJV)**

Hallelujah! Lord, thank you for being in control and in charge during such a time as this. We know that you have ordained those that lead us, but we ask that you take over the decisions of those who are making decisions for our country, because they do not make any sense. Help them, Lord God. Please take over, because we know that you are the King of Kings and the Lord of Lords. We know that your decisions are not made to harm us but to keep us safe and protected. Our leaders need correction, in Jesus' mighty name.

Help them to make the right choices and come together as a real, honest, sincere, trustworthy, safe, faithful, committed team, in Jesus' name. We command, rebuke, and come against the enemy for bringing confusion. I declare that everyone will pick up their cross, and let Jesus have His way in our lives. God delights in His children, and this is all part of His plan and purpose.

> *"Love the Lord your God with all your heart*
> *and with all your soul and with all your strength."*
> ***(Deuteronomy 6:5 NIV)***

Lord, help us to keep your commandments in our hearts. Thank you that your Word sets a pattern that helps us relate it to our daily lives. I declare that we will think constantly about your commandments and teach them to our children, living each day by the guidelines in your Word. Your first and greatest commandment is to love you with all of our hearts. Right now, in Jesus' mighty name, I declare that people will start obeying your commandments, turning to Christ, repenting, renouncing, confessing, and surrendering to you. I declare that everyone be turned to you today.

This is a new day, a new beginning, in Jesus' name. Have your way, Lord. We ask that you get us through this day and through this week, taking one step at a time. We surrender, asking you to do whatever you want to do, because you are good and in control.

Remove whatever will try to hinder our walk with you or bring worry or fear into our life, because you do not give us the spirit of fear but a spirit of love and a sound mind. Remove the old and fill us with the new, in Jesus' name.

Thank you that during times of trials and affliction, there is hope. Thank you for your great faithfulness.

> *"Because of the Lord's great love, we are not consumed, for His*
> *compassions never fail. They are new every morning, great*
> *is Your faithfulness. I say to myself, The Lord is my portion;*
> *therefore, I will wait for Him. The Lord is good to those whose*
> *hope is in Him, to the one who seeks Him. It is good to wait*
> *quietly for the salvation of the Lord."*
> ***(Lamentations 3:22-26 NIV)***

Father God, I know that we have all experienced your faithfulness. I pray that we will trust you day by day, because it will make us confident in your great promises for the future. I pray that because of your faithfulness, we will stay obedient, faithful, and committed, and seek you during these troubled times. I declare that we are willing to come under your discipline and learn what you want to teach us. You are the head of our lives. Thank you for loving us the way you do.

This season is hard for all of us but especially for our brothers and sisters battling addiction, sickness, and disease. Lord, we ask that you help them to realize that their struggle will not define their identity or worth. They are your children, called by your name, and set apart for your purpose. Show them that their chains have been broken. Lord, help those with addictions resist temptation so that they can embrace your fullness of life. Cover the sick, whose diseases may be overwhelming, with the blood of Jesus, and fill them with strength, peace, and healing upon their bodies, in Jesus' powerful name. Give them your strength to fight back, and place people in their lives who will support them. Protect their bodies, hearts, and minds. Shield them from temptation, sickness, and disease, and deliver them from evil, in Jesus' mighty name.

Thank you, Father God, that prayer is more powerful than our struggles and that we can fight our battles with prayer, knowing that we will always win. When the devil goes hard after us, we go harder; we pray and love with all we have because grace wins every time. Lord, heal and cover us because you are in control, and this too shall pass. Abba, thank you for placing your hands on us this morning and allowing your sons and daughters to see another day. We are so blessed, grateful, and thankful for who you are.

Thank you for being everywhere, Lord God, for we have nothing to fear. I pray that we surrender every area of our mind, will, and emotions to you. We know that the battle is not ours but yours. Remind us that our strength comes from you. I declare that we will not dare give up because the Lord our God will strengthen us and encourage through Christ Jesus our Lord. We are not alone; we are in this together and spiritually connected, with God on our side, right here in the midst of it all. Right now, we must give it to God, be still, be patient, and wait—because He is in control. And it all is in His timing, not ours! God doesn't ask us to stop living. He wants us to rise, strive, and never lose sight of the One who's above all. Family, nothing in heaven or on earth outshines our Almighty Lord God…how amazing and awesome is that? We praise you, honor you, and give you the glory…because you deserve it all.

*"My flesh and my heart may fail,*
*but God is the strength of my heart and my portion forever."*
***(Psalm 73:26 NIV)***

God's power is at work in all of us. Though our courage and strength may fail, we know that we will be raised to life to serve again. We have to thank and praise our Almighty God, because He is still using us, supplying, leading, and providing all of our needs. He is our security, and we must continue to cling to Him.

Thank you, Abba. We love you and appreciate you so much. We glorify you. You are our everything, and we ask you to use our life for your glory. In Jesus' name, I pray. Amen.

# Day 29
## PRAISE HIM FOR A FRESH TOUCH

Heavenly Father, we thank you for your Son Jesus. Lord Jesus, today is your day, and we want your will to be done. Whatever happens, hold our hands and let's face it together.

> *"I have said these things to you, that in Me you may have peace.*
> *In the world you will have tribulation.*
> *But take heart; I have overcome the world."*
> ***(John 16:33 NIV)***

Thank you, Jesus, that when we are in sync with you, we have nothing to worry about, because you give us peace and comfort in our relationship with you. Thank you for producing such great feelings in us. Your spirit living in us is so amazing, safe, and worry-free. Hallelujah! We love you and appreciate you. Thank you for who you are, breathing a fresh touch of goodness into your sons and daughters again. This is our time alone with you, and we ask that you have your way as we continue to bask in your presence, giving you permission to do whatever you want to do in and through us.

I pray that we take courage no matter what is going on around us. Help us to know that we are not alone. Thank you for not abandoning us. We must remember that the ultimate victory has already been won, and we can claim the peace of Christ in the most troublesome times. We are under God's authority. We are chosen believers, safe from Satan's power. We are set apart, and God is making us pure and holy, uniting us through His truth. Hallelujah! We praise you, Lord God. We honor and give you the glory. You are so good no matter what is going on. Thank you for loving us so much. We stand in awe of how powerful, good, faithful, worthy, and gracious you are. We are far from mighty without you Lord…but we are not without you. We are totally dependent on you, in Jesus' mighty name. Right now, we put on the full armor of God…the helmet of salvation, the breastplate of righteousness, the shield of faith, the belt of truth, the sword of the spirit that represents your Word, and the gospel of peace; our feet filled with the righteousness of Jesus Christ.

Lord, in the name of your Son Jesus, we ask that you use us for your purpose, because we need you and can do nothing without you. Thank you for drawing near to us as we communicate, seeking you before we do anything else and coming into agreement, in Jesus' mighty name. Thank you, Lord, for being with us.

> *"The Lord answered, 'I will be with you, and you will strike down all the Midianites together.'"*
> **(Judges 6:16 NIV)**

God told Gideon that He would be with him and He was, but Gideon made excuses, not knowing that God would want to work through him just like He wants to work through us. God tested Gideon's faith and commitment. After a while, Gideon took a great risk by following God's higher law, which specifically forbids idol worship. The enemy got mad because Gideon followed God…but God was in control and in charge, just as He is now. He is the King of Kings and the Lord of Lords, and we are called to serve Him in specific ways. No matter what is happening, He wants us to follow His commandments. He wants us to do incredible things because He also calls us to depend on Him.

As we are in the kingdom, it requires utter dependence on God. He will give us the strength, tools, and peace that we need. If we show Him our limitations, it implies that He does not know all about us. I pray that we will spend our time doing what God wants us to do, without making excuses. Thank you, God, for having your way.

Lord, our world is broken and dysfunctional. Bad things are happening to good people and sin is all around us in such a time as this. Father God, we know that it's hard to imagine on earth as it is in heaven.

> *"This, then, is how you should pray: 'Our Father in heaven, hallowed be your name, your kingdom come, your will be done on earth as it is in heaven. Give us today our daily bread. Forgive us our debts, as we also forgive our debtors. And lead us not into temptation but deliver us from the evil one.'"*
> **(Matthew 6:9-13 NIV)**

Thank you, Abba, for your prayer that Jesus gave to His disciples. We praise you for your work in this world, for supplying our needs, and for helping us in our daily struggles. Lord, we ask that your perfect purpose be accomplished in this world today because you are our sustainer and provider. Lord, your Kingdom is a place of perfect justice and truth; and at the end of time, all things will be set right. Injustices will be made right, sins will be forgiven, and illnesses will be healed, in Jesus' mighty name. The truth is that even though everything seems out of control right now, Jesus has never left us, and He never will. I declare that we will pray confidently, knowing that we can surrender all to God. That is where He wants our heart. He wants us to be at peace with Him, confident that whatever happens during this time, the day can be handled together.

> *"I have told you these things, so that in me you may have peace. In this world you will have trouble. But take heart! I have overcome the world."*
> **(John 16:33 NIV)**

Hallelujah!

You are so amazing, Abba. Thank you for your Son Jesus, fully placed at the center of our universe; we can be confident that He has overcome the world. With that confidence firmly planted in our heart, we can face anything the world and our circumstances bring us because you are still in control and in charge. We must trust you, walking by faith and not by sight. Praying, reading our Bible, coming into agreement, waiting, and being patient, still, brave, kind, thankful, and happy. Our worries are few, but our blessings are many. Today is your day, Lord Jesus! Let your will be done. We are not alone. We are in this together and are spiritually connected. Thank you, Abba, for who you are, in Jesus' name. Amen.

# Day 30
## THANK HIM FOR SPIRITUAL VISION

*Eternal Holy God our Father,*

We come before you in the name of Jesus your Son. Forgive us for our sins. Thank you for your presence and that you are right here, covering and shielding us, your sons and daughters. Thank you for loving us, for walking with us, and for caring about the smallest details in this world and in our lives. We know that you are still in control, taking care of everything because you said that you will never leave us nor forsake us.

Thank you for waking each of us up this morning as you have had your angels watching and surrounding us. We give you the glory, honor, and praise because we are still here alive, breathing, talking, walking, listening to our Father God, and doing what you want to do in our lives. As we come into agreement, we ask that you be in the midst of it all.

> *"Ask and it will be given to you; seek and you will find; knock and the door will be opened to you."*
> ***(Matthew 7:7 NIV)***

Thank you for your Word, Lord. Thank you that we can trust you, because you created life in us so that we have nothing to worry about. Worrying will hamper our efforts for today; so, we rest, knowing that you are in control and know the future. Thank you, Abba, for not ignoring us…because we have been depending on you. I declare that we will not worry because it shows a lack of faith and understanding of you. I pray that we live one day at a time because it will keep us from being consumed with worry.

Father God, you know every decision that we need to make and every challenge that we face. Forgive us if we have tried to figure anything out on our own. We need your Holy Spirit to give us strength, wisdom, and direction. Thank you, Abba, for who you are! Father God, our spiritual vision is our capacity to see clearly what you want us to do, and to see the world from your point of view. I declare that our eyes will be fixed on you. Thank you, Lord, for still being in control and never leaving nor forsaking your sons and daughters.

You are glorious and gracious and so good. Lord, even though life appears out of control, you are in control and in charge of it all. We are spiritually connected with you, Father God, right here in the midst of it all. We know that seasons change, but your love remains. I pray we remember that you are not withholding your promises, knowing that your timeline is different from ours. Lord, our waiting may be actually preparing us for the plans and purposes you have for us. Waiting helps us focus on your faithfulness. Thank you that it has not changed.

God is patiently protecting and providing for us. His presence is evidence for us to look back on what He has done for us, and this will help us hold on to hope. Hoping in God is never wasted because the One who conquered death is still in control, and He's always at work in our waiting. Thank you, Jesus. We will trust in you, standing firm in our faith.

> *"The Lord Your God is with you; He is mighty to save.*
> *He will take great delight in you, He will quiet you with His*
> *love, He will rejoice over you with singing."*
> **(Zephaniah 3:17 NIV)**

Thank you, Abba, for giving us gladness. Only you can make us truly happy. I declare that we will allow you to be with us and will be obedient to you. When we follow your commands and obey you, you rejoice over us with singing.

That is amazing. I declare that we will draw close to the source of happiness by obeying you in Jesus' mighty name.

> *"Give thanks to the Lord, for He is good; His love endures forever."*
> **(Psalm 118:1 NIV)**

Thank you for loving us so much. You are alive. You are thinking about us and caring for us and we should put you first in our lives every day. I declare that we will.

> *"Praise the Lord, all you nations; extol Him, all you people. For great is His love toward us, and the faithfulness of the Lord endures forever. Praise the Lord."*
> **(Psalm 117:1-2 NIV)**

Let us draw God closer to us and us closer to God as we meditate on this Psalm. It gives us reasons for praising God…His great love toward us, and His faithfulness that endures forever. If God did nothing else for us, He would still be worthy of our highest praise. He is unchanging and it gives us security and confidence in God's eternal love. Hallelujah!

Lord, we know that many are lost and following their own will, not realizing that it is time for them to get their life right with you by coming to Jesus. Lord Jesus, we pray that you will open the door to these lost souls and stand against the many adversaries of the gospel. *(1 Corinthians 16:9)*. We pray that you will circumcise their hearts so that they will love you. *(Deuteronomy 30:6)*. We pray that they will know the truth, and the truth shall set them free *(John 8:32)*.

Lord Jesus, open the door that will allow us to speak your gospel to them. You are able to do exceedingly, abundantly above all that we ask or think, according to the power that works in us. Jesus, make a way out of the wilderness for them, and lift up your supernatural ways upon them and give them peace.

We thank you Jesus for commanding us to pray for lost souls that is a priority for every Christian believer, focusing on others instead of ourselves in our prayers. That we are to love our neighbors as we love ourselves *(Matthew 22:39)*. Thank you, Lord, for your words.

Lord, we know that many are not feeling well. We lift them up before you for supernatural healing, in Jesus' mighty name. Give them strength to be strong today; strength to be strong in their fight. You are their comforter, Lord, and we place your power in them. Send someone their way to speak over them because they need it Lord. We command every pain to leave their bodies. Touch them with your comfort, your peace, and your goodness. They are not alone because you are their covering. Jesus, comfort their minds, bodies, and spirits. You are the true peace; grant them an awareness of your presence. Lord, ease every pain. Have your way, because you are the supernatural healer. We plead the blood of Jesus over your people by the power of His name. Thank you for drawing near to our cries and knowing that we need you. Thank you that we are not alone, and we come together, still spiritually connected in such a time as this. You get all the glory. Thank you. In Jesus' name, Amen.

# Day 31
## A Prayer for the Light

Oh Lord Almighty, as you have taught us to call the evening, the morning, and the noonday as one day, and you have made the sun to know it's going down, dispel the darkness of our hearts…that through your brightness we may know you to be the true God and eternal light, living and reigning forever and ever. Thank you, Lord God, for you are worthy, faithful, good, and so much more to us. We praise you; we glorify you because you deserve it. Without you, we would not be here today, for you sent your only Son Jesus to die for our sins and save us. Lord, we ask that you forgive us for the sins that we commit. We know that only Jesus is perfect. Thank you for thinking of us. Heavenly Father, our prayer is that your will be done, in Jesus' mighty name.

Steer our intentions to align with your righteous will. May all glory be lifted up to you. We trust you for you are the King of Kings and the Lord of Lords. Father God, keep love at the forefront of our minds tonight and always, as the guiding light for all we set out to accomplish and celebrate. Lord God, we praise you for this day and your purpose for it. Reset our agendas as we sit in your presence. We ask that you give us a grateful heart so that we will be thankful for all things: our daily provision, food, clothing, shelter, health, our families, friends, and co-workers, and those who you bring into our lives to both love us and test us; knowing that they are from your loving hand to enable our growth. We must practice the same attitude as Christ.

Today, examine your attitudes, motives, and relationships. Ask God to forgive those things that the Holy Spirit helps you identify as sin in your life. Thank Him for freeing you from guilt, and ask Him to fill you with the fullness of the Holy Spirit. Thank you for who you are and for drawing near to us, as we are coming into agreement and believing your will to be done, in Jesus' name. We declare that breakthroughs will happen today. Let there be supernatural healing and strength today, in the name of Jesus Christ. Thank you for showing up and showing out.

God remains the same yesterday, today, and forever. He is still with us, listening to us, and extending His peace to our troubled hearts. I pray that we will worship more and worry less, in Jesus' name. I declare that we will stand firm in our faith and trust Him, because He is still in control.

> *"Blessed are the poor in spirit, for theirs is the kingdom of heaven. Blessed are those who mourn, for they will be comforted. Blessed are the meek, for they will inherit the earth. Blessed are those who hunger and thirst for righteousness, for they will be filled. Blessed are the merciful, for they will be shown mercy. Blessed are the pure in heart, for they will see God. Blessed are the peacemakers, for they will be called sons of God. Blessed are those who are persecuted because of righteousness. Blessed are you when people insult you, persecute you and falsely say all kinds of evil against you because of me. Rejoice and be glad, because great is your reward in heaven, for in the same way they persecuted the prophets who were before you."*
> **(Matthew 5:3-11 NIV)**

Thank you for your goodness in such a time as this. Thank you for your hope and joy—the deepest form of happiness—and for guiding us to follow Jesus no matter what the cost. If we live for you, we will glow like lights, showing others what you are like.

I declare that we as believers will not shut our light off from the rest of the world and that we will be the light when we enter into the darkness. We will shine like Christ to His glory.

> *"The Lord is my light and my salvation; whom shall I fear? The Lord is the strength of my life; of whom shall I be afraid?"*
> **(Psalm 27:1 NIV)**

Thank you for being so faithful and worthy to us. We appreciate and love you. You deserve all the glory and honor. Thank you for helping us today to have hope for the future. I declare right now that we will have faith over fear and peace over panic and that our prayers are more powerful than our struggles. Thank you, Jesus, for thinking of us on your way to the Cross.

Father, we ask that you surround us with guardian angels. Protect us from the evil of this world. Place supernatural healing angels around us, keeping us safe and healthy in Jesus' mighty name. Amen.

> *"These things I have spoken unto you, that in me ye might have peace. In the world ye shall have tribulation, but be of good cheer, I have overcome the world."*
> **(John 16:33 KJV)**

Being in sync with Christ will produce peace and comfort in your life.

> *"Therefore, if any man be in Christ, he is a new creature: old things are passed away; behold all things are become new."*
> **(2 Corinthians 5:17 NIV)**

> *"If you remain in me and my words remain in you, ask whatever you wish, and it will be done for you."*
> **(John 15:7 NIV)**

Jesus will give us the strength that we need when we come to Him and live for Him. We cannot allow small problems to get in the way. We must remember that He will give us supernatural strength.

> *"For all the promises of God in him are yea, and in him Amen, unto the glory of God by us."*
> **(2 Corinthians 1:20 KJV)**

We can trust God to keep His promises. When we are His representative, that is when others can trust us.

Everything is fulfilled in Christ.

According to these Scriptures, we can find...

- Peace
- New life
- Answered prayers
- God's promises

Father God, for those of us who are not living for you, we may be missing these things. We know that it is not because you don't want us to have them; we have just been looking for peace, new life, answered prayers, and your promises in the wrong places:

- Our *name*
- Our *money*
- Our *job*
- Our *title*
- Our *friends*
- Our *family*
- Our *success*

Lord, we ask that you help us get out of our own desires and into Jesus!

Jesus, we thank you for faithfully dying for us, for being faithful in your ministry, for never sinning, and for faithfully interceding for us. Because you are faithful to us, I decree and declare that we will be faithful in our ministry too.

We thank you, Lord, for being our Redeemer. I believe that there is going to be a breakthrough because where there is faith, there are miracles happening. Lord, bring conviction on us. We command the devil to release your people and we declare salvation, in the name of Jesus. We may not be able to lay hands on them physically, but we lay hands on them right now in the Spirit.

Jesus, help those who are not saved. You died in their place and rose again from the grave to make them new and to prepare them to live in your presence.

Come into their lives, take control, and forgive them of their sins. Help them to place their trust in you alone for their salvation, and accept your free gift of eternal life.

I decree and declare that we would have faith that our God works. This is all for His plan and His purpose. He does not make mistakes—He knows what He is doing. He wants to bring us to a place of dependence on Him; to encourage us to pray, change our life, and clean ourselves up.

We thank you, Abba, for having your way, for doing what you knew was right, and for protecting us from those things that only you know. In Jesus' name we pray. Amen.

# Day 32
## A Prayer for Healing

*Heavenly Father,* we come before you in the name of your Son Jesus Christ. We thank you for another day; for waking us up and breathing into your sons and daughters again. Thank you for carrying us through another month…because of you, we have made it this far. Lord, we pray that this month will be blessed with wisdom, peace, ideas, opportunities, mental and financial growth, and supernatural spiritual health. Lord God, take us beyond our own expectations. We pray that this will be a month of healing. I decree and declare supernatural healing, in Jesus' mighty name. We declare that we give this world back to God.

I pray that we would shut off the "autopilot" and make room for a word from you. I pray that we would trust more in you and your ability to speak than we do in our (in)ability to listen. I pray that we will incline our ears and eyes to hear from you and we declare that your Word will have an effect on us, in Jesus' mighty name.

We declare and decree that there will be true understanding and walking in the Spirit, because your Word will pierce through our hearts and drop us to our knees to worship you whole-heartedly. Right now, God, draw near to us. Wake us up to start our day seeking you and basking in your presence.

Lord, your law is perfect and right. You are the Living Word from the beginning of time, and your Word has brought light and life. What you command surely will come to pass. Lord, you said that despite our spiritual failure, you will show mercy. We ask that you bring your sons and daughters back from captivity and restore us, in Jesus' name.

> *"It pleased the Lord for the sake of His righteousness to make His law great and glorious."*
> **(Isaiah 42:21 NIV)**

Thank you for who you are. Gracious, faithful, worthy; you are everything, Abba. Jehovah-Jireh, the Lord, our provider. Yahweh. Lord, let us just take a moment to thank you your goodness. You know we are always praying for others and for ourselves. We want to say thank you, for your name is amazing and powerful. God Almighty. Living God. Creator of everything that exists. Yahweh, you are powerful, revealing yourself as the most sacred and distinctive. We appreciate you so much and are so grateful. We should have no fear, worry, or doubt…because you are the strength of our life.

> *"The Lord is my light and my salvation—whom shall I fear? The Lord is the stronghold of my life—of whom shall I be afraid?"*
> **(Psalm 27:1 NIV)**

We are blessed. At this moment, we need to thank God for how blessed we all are. He put us on the earth, and though it will never be a straight path that we are on, He put us here for a reason.

Father God, right now we thank you for our families, true friends, life, health, and strength. I decree and declare that we will never blame you for anything. I pray we remember that you have blessed us with something to renew our faith and to remind us that we have a purpose. I pray that we will look with our heart and not our eyes! I declare that we will never lose our faith because where there is faith, miracles happen. Father God, we just thank you for allowing us a moment to honor you and show you respect, giving you the glory because you deserve it all, and without you not one of us would be here today. We love you, Abba. We are you children…how amazing and awesome is that! We have the privilege of talking to our Daddy God. Hallelujah. Tears of joy, knowing you are not yet finished. We are all yours, and you have called each of us by name. Thank you, Almighty God.

Abba, your light shines through us. Living for you is amazing because your spirit is powerful. Help us to become an element of surprise, in Jesus' mighty name. Fill us with passion and consistency. Fill us with compassion for others, and let us have a boldness for our lives. I declare that we will stand firm and be well built, in Jesus' name. Amen.

# Day 33
## THANK HIM FOR AN ETERNAL PERSPECTIVE

*"O Lord, I will direct my song and my prayer unto you and will look up."*
**(Psalm 5:3b KJV)**

Good morning, Lord. Thank you for waking us up. We thank you for a blessed weekend breathing in us. We are still alive here on earth for a reason and a purpose; your plans Abba, not ours. You are so faithful and worthy, Lord. Thank you. You get the glory for it is about you. Have your way, Lord. Remind us that prayer holds the power to center us and guide us into the flow of the day, and helps us to keep an eternal perspective amid life's chaos, reminding us of your power in both good and bad times.

*"Rejoice always; pray continually; give thanks in all circumstances for this is God's will for you in Christ Jesus."*
**(1 Thessalonians 5:16-18 NIV)**

Lord God, help us to know that our joy, prayers, and thankfulness should not fluctuate with our circumstances. I declare that we will obey, be joyful, pray continually, and give thanks in Jesus' mighty name. Thank you that when we do your will, we find it easy to be joyful and thankful. Hallelujah! It is an incredible way to start the day…basking in your presence and seeking you, communicating with you. You are the giver of life, and I pray that every time we awake with a new morning, we do so with excitement, knowing that it is important that we turn to you and offer up our gratitude. We are grateful for the beauty of the sun and your creation. I pray that we will always be overjoyed by the wonders around us, thanking you for our life. Despite what goes on around us, there is nothing we can do except pray, read your Word, and come into agreement, standing in the gap and waiting on your timing, not ours. We are thankful for your presence and for the good that you have been accomplishing. We will not fear or waver Lord, because you are still in control.

*"Therefore, what God has joined together, let man not separate."*
***(Mark 10:9 KJV)***

With everything going on Lord, let us not give up our spiritual connection. I declare that we will be effective, faithful prayer warriors; praying according to your will without reservation or doubt and expecting your goodness. During these prayers, I declare and decree that we will be ready to go to prayer when we are alone. We will be confident, bold, courageous, and able to stand in the ranks, because you give us your full armor. We will stay alert in the spirit.

*"Lord be gracious to us; we long for you.*
*Be our strength every morning, our salvation in time of distress."*
***(Isaiah 33:2 NIV)***

Father God, may we have faith over fear, and peace over panic in such a time as this. We are waiting for you to deliver us from oppression. We trust in you, the Ruler and the Creator of the universe. We walk by faith and not by sight, for the joy of the Lord is our strength. *(Nehemiah 8:10)*.

We ask for comfort with a quest for your supernatural strength, healing, peace, joy, wisdom and discernment that we can only seek from you. Thank you, Jesus, for your comfort and strength, and for guiding and drawing near to us, your sons and daughters. Please be with us throughout this day, and help us navigate whatever comes our way. More importantly, help us to live out our lives in a way that is honoring you. We put our trust in you; show us the way we should go. Use us for your purpose, Lord, not our desires.

Lord, help us as parents. Remind us to have important talks with our children at such a time as this, because it is important that they know what goes on in life when they awake and can understand right from wrong. Thank you, Lord, for the wonderful parents that are here on earth. Help us, Lord, because we need you.

Father God, have mercy on us. Guard our homes, our families, our friends, and our relatives, in Jesus' name. You are the God of power and glory; send your angels to fight the invisible enemy. Let this be a new day where we see you in all that we do. We are blessed, thankful, and grateful.

Lord, ease our minds. We will be patient and still, not rushing our lives but trusting that you know best. Thank you, Jesus, for who you are. We love and appreciate you. Father God, if our faith remains strong even while surrounded by life's difficulties, we will continue to experience your untold blessings.

> *"Blessed is the man who perseveres under trial, because when he has stood the test, he will receive the crown of life that God has promised to those who love Him."*
> **(James 1:12 NIV)**

We must have confidence, serve with compassionate hearts, and speak carefully. We should have giving hearts, be concerned about sharing God's truth—the gospel of Jesus Christ—and helping those in need. Thank you, Father, for helping us to show your truth of how to live for you; faithful and committed, obeying your commands and following your lead.

I pray that we will stay faithful even under pressure. Nothing evil comes from you, for you are good all the time. We thank you for being real, powerful, and unstoppable. We thank you for shining your light on us. Thank you for your Son Jesus, dying for us our sins. Thank you for your grace, mercy, and forgiveness. Have your way in our lives, that we live each day, honoring and obeying you. Amen.

# Day 34
## PRAISE HIM IN AGREEMENT

*Good morning, Heavenly Father.* Thank you for waking us up this morning to another glorious day of believing in dramatic change. We know you are not finished with us yet and that there is still much you want us to do. Have your way, in Jesus' name. We give you the glory and the honor. Move in this place, for we know that you are in the midst when two or three are gathered in your name.

Thank you for drawing near to us. In the name of the Father and the Son and the Holy Spirit, we come together in agreement this morning, requesting our prayers, works, joys, and sufferings of this day; prayers for others along with ourselves, and an essential part of a good prayer life with help from you, Lord Jesus. I declare that our prayer life will draw us closer to you like never before by expressing our love for you, thanking you for your blessings, and offering you everything about our day. Thank you, Lord, for who you are. We pray that your will be done and believe for breakthroughs, in the precious wonderful name of Jesus Christ. Hallelujah! We will never stop praying. We know, Lord God, that you can change things in an instant, because we believe in miracles.

> *"Therefore, brothers, since we have confidence to enter the Most Holy Place by the blood of Jesus, by a new and living way opened for us through the curtain, that is, His body, and since we have a great priest over the house of God, let us draw near to God with a sincere heart in full assurance of faith, having our hearts sprinkled to cleanse us from a guilty conscience and having our bodies washed with pure water. Let us hold unswervingly to*

*the hope we profess, for He who promised is faithful. And let us consider how we may spur one another on toward love and good deeds. Let us not give up meeting together, as some are in the habit of doing, but let us encourage one another and all the more as you see the day approaching."*
**(Hebrews 10:19-25 NIV)**

Hallelujah! Thank you, Jesus, for speaking to us. We have significant privileges associated with our new life in you, including personal access to God through you. I declare and decree that our faith is rising, and that we will not doubt but will deepen our relationship with you in such a time as this because you are still in control and there is nothing that we can do except pray, trust, believe, and walk by faith and not by sight. Hallelujah. It is okay for us to enjoy encouragement and help from one another. It is okay for us to continue to worship and praise God because we are free and have victory in Christ Jesus.

*"The joy of the Lord is your strength."*
**(Nehemiah 8:10b NIV)**

When we neglect our meetings, we are giving up the encouragement and help of other Christians; but as we are still spiritually connected, we are strengthening our faith and one another in the Lord. There will be many spiritual struggles and even times of persecution, but difficulties should never be excuses for us missing church. You are global now…how amazing and wonderful is that! Father God, we thank you and praise you for turning evil into your goodness. What the devil has tried to use for evil, you have changed into good. We are kneeling before you Abba, worshiping, praising, and shouting before you.

*"It is written: 'As surely as I live,' says the Lord, 'every knee will bow before me; every tongue will acknowledge God.'"*
**(Romans 14:11 NIV)**

*"That at the name of Jesus every knee should bow, in heaven and on earth and under the earth, and every tongue confess that Jesus Christ is Lord, to the glory of God the Father."*
**(Philippians 2:10-11 NIV)**

> *"By myself I have sworn, my mouth has uttered in all integrity*
> *a word that will not be revoked: Before me every knee will bow;*
> *by me every tongue will swear."*
> **(Isaiah 45:23 NIV)**

Hallelujah! Thank you, Almighty Lord, for your powerful words. You are the King of Kings and the Lord of Lords.

As difficulties arise, we should make an even greater effort to be faithful in our spiritual connection and attendance. We come against the lies and works of the enemy because our God is awesome. He can move mountains. He can heal us in the valleys and hide us from the rain. I declare that no matter what is going on, we will rise up, take courage, and do what our Father God wants us to do. We come against busyness; we will wake up every morning, seeking God and being obedient when the spirit moves, and we will worship no matter what is going on or how we feel. With God, all things are possible.

I declare that our walk with Christ will be our number one priority, in Jesus' mighty name.

> *"In all your ways acknowledge Him*
> *and He will make your paths straight."*
> **(Proverbs 3:6 NIV)**

God knows what is best for us and is a better judge of what we think we want than we are! We must trust Him completely in every choice we make.

> *"I the Lord do not change."*
> **(Malachi 3:6a NIV)**

I pray that we rely on Jesus, because He will see us through. Father God please keep us rooted firmly in you as our immovable foundation. Keep us in your Word, and keep us in constant communication through prayer and with you, in Jesus' name.

Thank you, Father God, for your amazing powerful words, and for your compassion, power, grace, love, authority, and dominion over all of us. You are always speaking through and to us; we are yours, Abba. We are children of God, and our God's words will never disappear. His Word speaks through us when we keep it in our hearts.

Thank you, Abba, for being so faithful and worthy, and for loving us the way you do. Have your way, in Jesus' mighty name. Amen.

# Day 35
## PRAISE HIM FOR HIS AUTHORITY

Almighty Lord God, Jehovah-Jireh, we thank you for an amazing, shining morning, and for waking us up and breathing in us again. We invite you to join us in our request before you because we trust in you for your will to be done, not ours. I pray that our words align with your words, as we come into agreement, locking hands because we are spiritually connected, in Jesus' mighty name. We are seeking you and communicating with you, Creator and Ruler of the universe. Have your way Lord.

Lord God, bless this day, and keep us safe from harm. I pray that today will be a better day than yesterday. Pick us up and hold us in your loving arms. Protect us from the pressures of the day, and remove the heaviness from our hearts. Command every negative thought and every stronghold—anything that is not of you Lord—to leave, in Jesus' name. We speak strength, rest, joy, peace, excitement, gladness, and rejoicing to come back into our bodies, into our lives, into our paths, in Jesus' mighty name.

- We receive *strength*.
- We receive *rest*.
- We receive *joy*.
- We receive *peace*.
- We receive *excitement*.
- We receive *gladness*.
- We receive *rejoicing*.

We speak it. We *declare* it, in Jesus' mighty name. Hallelujah! God, you have given us the authority and power to trample on serpents and scorpions and over all the power of the enemy, who is always trying and is against us, but nothing can hurt us. *(Luke 10:19)*

> *"'No weapon forged against you will prevail, and you will refute every tongue that accuses you. This is the heritage of the servants of the Lord, and this is their vindication from me,' declares the Lord."*
> ***(Isaiah 54:17 NIV)***

Things may attempt to distract us, come against us, and take us down, but that does not mean that they will happen. You, Daddy God, have given us what we need to prevail and be victorious. Hallelujah! Thank you, Jesus, that we have the victory.

We declare breakthrough right now, in Jesus' mighty name. We have risen up using the authority God has given us to use through Jesus, because we just speak to those mountains to be removed…we *command* those mountains to be removed…and it is so. Hallelujah!

Just smile right now, wherever you are, praising our Lord Almighty because He is our good Father. He is still in control no matter what has been going on. We have been walking by faith, not by sight, trusting in God because He is the King of Kings and the Lord of Lords. Hallelujah!

We are women and men of faith. God has inspired us with the knowledge that together, we can handle anything, in Jesus' mighty name. Whenever there are deep waters, we remember that we do not have to worry because God is with us. We do not have to tremble or be afraid because there is no other God besides Him, no other rock, not one.

> *"I made you, I formed you in the womb, I will help You, do not ever be afraid, just trust me, do not give up, I got this, I chose you, I appointed you."*
> ***(Isaiah 42:2, 44:2, 44:8 NIV)***

*"I ordained you. I anointed you and you are My child. I called your name two thousand years before all this was going to happen, and I want you to trust Me,*

*your Daddy God. I am the First and the Last, apart from Me, there is no God. I want, and I need you to be proud that you belong to Me, your Papa, your Abba, your everything, in Jesus' mighty name. No matter what is going on today, I need you My daughter, My son, to be unashamed and delighted, and to let everyone know about your intimate relationship with Me, your Heavenly Father God."*

God has said that since we invited Him to be with us, He has been protecting us, covering us, and shielding us…because we are His children. Hallelujah!

Thank you, Jesus. You are a good Father, and we praise you. We lift you up high, for you deserve all the honor, all the glory.

Lord, thank you for loving us the way you do. We appreciate you. We magnify and glorify you. Father God, we ask that you help those who are in need, because you know everything that goes on. Lord, for those of us who are separated from our loved ones, bring comfort to us. Wrap your arms around us. Allow us to feel a warm touch from the Almighty God. We pray supernatural healing and we plead the blood of Jesus over your people; our families, friends, and coworkers. Cause your face to shine on us in Jesus' name. Cover this nation, Lord, because it needs you. These countries need you, Lord God; they may not think so, but they do. Lord, we know that one prayer can change any situation. Let your will be done, in Jesus' mighty name. Have your way, Abba.

Heavenly Father, thank you for the life-changing blessings that are coming our way, in Jesus' mighty name. Thank you in advance. We know and believe that you have great things in store for us. We surrender everything to you. As the devil has been going hard, I declare that we will go harder by staying connected, praying, staying in your Word, and waiting quietly and patiently, trusting in God. Walking by faith not by sight and showing love with everything we have, because grace wins every time.

Father God, we pray that today is filled with connection, love, joy, growth, breakthrough, closer families, and deeper connection with you. Help us to remember the closer we walk with you, the less room there is for anything to come between us. Thank you, Lord, for who you are. We bless you and love you. We pray this all in Jesus' name. Amen.

# Day 36
## PRAISE HIM IN THE WAITING

Heavenly Father, we thank you for this beautiful, wonderful morning that you woke us up to. For this is the day you have made, let us rejoice in it. We are still here, alive and breathing. Thank you, Jesus. Thank you, Father, for who you are. The light of the world. You are everything, and you are everywhere, and we thank you, appreciate you, and love you, Lord God. It is all about you and not us.

Lord, you are our light and our salvation; we do not have to fear. You are the strength of our life and we do not have to be afraid of anything. Hallelujah! Thank you, Lord God, that we can conquer fear by using the bright liberating light of you who brings salvation. I pray that we have confidence, knowing that we will see the goodness of the Lord no matter what.

> *"Wait for the Lord; be strong and take heart and wait for the Lord."*
> **(Psalm 27:14 NIV)**

We thank you Abba for your powerful words. We know that prayer simply means for us to talk honestly to you and listen for you to speak. Thank you for drawing near to your sons and daughters. Lord, we know waiting is not easy, but we know with you in control and in charge, remaining still and patient is worth the wait.

> *"I say to myself, 'The Lord is my portion; therefore, I will wait for Him.' The Lord is good to those whose hope is in Him, to the one who seeks Him; it is good to wait quietly for the salvation of the Lord."*
> **(Lamentations 3:24-26 NIV)**

Thank you for who you are and that we can keep our hope in the midst of whatever goes on around us. Thank you for your promises of restoration and blessings. I pray that we trust in your faithfulness, day by day, making us confident in your great promises for the future. We ask that you refresh, renew, and teach us like never before, in Jesus' name.

I pray that we make good use of our waiting by discovering what you may be trying to teach us. Thank you, Jesus.

Lord, as we are in agreement women and men of faith, we lift up our nation before you, in the name of Jesus Christ. Lord forgive us and forgive our nation. Forgive those who think that they don't need to apologize for their mistakes, Abba. We pray that people will run to you and have faith in what you are telling us. We command people to turn to you, in the mighty name of Jesus. Please show people that their way is not your plan for us and that better times are coming if they believe in Jesus' mighty name. We command this nation to turn to you, in Jesus' name.

Thank you, God, for who you are, drawing near as we lift up our prayers to you. Bless America through these uncertain times that we find ourselves in. We command prayer of every single person in this nation to start seeking God's presence. Hallelujah! Have your way in this day. Protect us from the pressures of the day, and remove the heaviness from our hearts, in Jesus' name.

Father, thank you that you are with us through the twists and turns of life and that wherever we go, you have promised to be with us and have given us your assurance that your presence will accompany us to lead and to guide, to protect and to help. Father God, as this day has already started for many, we ask that you join us on this journey today and travel with your people, in Jesus' name. We pray that we will be kept by the power of God in the unity of the spirit through the bond of peace and that this may be a journey where you are lifted up in everyone's thoughts and prayers. Thank you, Holy Spirit, for speaking, and may it refresh us for a new day. Help us to remember that you are taking care of us, but we have to make the right decisions in life, using common sense, not rushing anything, and not going ahead of you, Father God. I pray for discernment, Lord, for us to hear from you. Help us to relax, to be patient and still and trust in you, in Jesus' name. Amen.

## Closing Prayer

Thank you, Lord, that in all things we may come to you and offer our prayers and petitions to you, knowing that you hear and answer all of your children. Let today be the day that great decisions are being made, both in this nation and in our lives. Let us move past fear, and go in the direction we know you are leading us, in Jesus' name. Give us more of your glory today. Fill us up, and help us to entrust all of our cares to you, because we know that you have the means to turn everything around, in Jesus' mighty name. Thank you for loving us and having our back. We glorify you. I declare that today will be a stress-free, joyful, peaceful, hopeful, and loving kind of day.

Lord, I declare that we put everything in your hands today: our families, our health, our home, our fears, and whatever else we need to cast to you, in Jesus' name. Thank you, Abba, for carrying our burdens.

Stay encouraged; and if no one encourages you, then encourage yourself in the Lord! We pray all this, in Jesus' name. Amen.

# Day 37
## THANK HIM FOR YOUR CHALLENGES

Almighty Heavenly Father, thank you for waking us up this morning. You are so faithful and worthy. We give you the glory, and we thank you for not being finished with us yet. Lord, forgive us for our sins. We thank you for your forgiveness. Father, before we begin our day, we want to say we love and appreciate you so much. You thought about each of us two thousand years ago, and you called each of us by name. We are your sons and daughters, and we thank you for your Son Jesus.

> *"Going a little farther He fell to the ground and prayed that if possible, the hour might pass from Him. 'Abba, Father,' He said, 'everything is possible for you. Take this cup from Me. Yet not what I will, but what You will.'"*
> ***(Mark 14:35-36 NIV)***

Hallelujah! Jesus, we thank you for reaffirming your desire to do what God wanted you to do. Thank you for your prayer highlights; for the terrible suffering that you had to endure. Thank you for enduring the agony because you had to take on the sins of the whole world. This cup was the agony of alienation from your Father at the Cross.

Thank you, Jesus, for being the sinless Son of God who took our sins and was separated for a while from your Father so that we could be eternally saved. Hallelujah! How amazing you are, Jesus, for thinking of us on your way to that

Cross as you carried it, beaten and suffering, dragging it with the strength that you had. You didn't care because each one of us was in your heart and mind. Jesus, we thank you for suffering for us. Thank you, Lord, for your Word and for the wisdom to apply it to our situation.

> *"Did not the Christ have to suffer these things and then enter His glory? He told them, 'This is what is written: the Christ will suffer and rise again from the dead the third day, and repentance and forgiveness of sins will be preached in His name to all nations, beginning at Jerusalem.'"*
> **(Luke 24:26, 46-47 NIV)**

Hallelujah!

This is how much God loved us. Two thousand years ago, before we were even formed in the womb, God already knew what He was going to do. The Word of God is to open our minds to understand the Scriptures. The Holy Spirit is so amazing that when we believed, we were marked with His Spirit. The Holy Spirit wants to help us by opening our mind to understand, giving us the needed insight to put God's Word into action in our lives. Hallelujah!

Luke wrote to the Greek-speaking world. He wanted them to know that the message of God's love and forgiveness should go to all the world. We must never ignore the worldwide scope of the gospel. God want all the world to hear the good news of salvation. We have to thank Him for choosing us, appointing us, and ordaining us. Hallelujah!

We thank you, Abba, for being so gracious and for loving us the way that you do. Even though we don't deserve *anything*, you give us *everything*. Lord, help us to appreciate when opportunities like this arise. That during such a time as this, you have been preparing us and working in each of us. I pray that we accept the peace from you, knowing that you long for us; we are your creation, marked with your image. Even when we struggle with issues outside of our control and when we make active choices, we are worth it—because our Creator said so. We thank you, Lord, that when we receive your grace and forgiveness wholeheartedly and experience your great love, it inspires deep thankfulness.

Thank you, Abba, for creating us. We honor you. We declare that we will take great care of our temple, because you made us—mind, heart, and body. We pray that we will protect it and use it to drive us into a deeper relationship with you. We declare that we will let others know that what they do not deserve is available, and it makes living so good, in Jesus' mighty name. Thank you, Lord, for your daily reminders of your love.

We thank you, Lord, for who you are. We praise you because all glory goes to you.

> *"May your father and mother rejoice;*
> *may she who gave you birth be joyful!"*
> **(Proverbs 23:25 NIV)**

> *"Many women do noble things, but you surpass them all. Charm*
> *is deceptive, and beauty is fleeting; but a woman who fears the*
> *Lord is to be praised. Give her the reward she has earned,*
> *and let her works bring her praise at the city gate."*
> **(Proverbs 31:29-31 NIV)**

Father God, we thank you for every mother who has worked so hard, cared for others, had concerns for the poor, shown great wisdom in handling money, feared you, shown respect to their spouse, made good decisions, and lived according to your ideals. Thank you for helping us to raise our children well. Right now, we just appreciate and love our mothers. We applaud them and thank them for being who they are.

Do not let your failures define you. God will use a willing and humble heart for great things. Sometimes, things go wrong for the right reasons. When we start doing what's right, remember that healthy things *grow*, growing things *change*, change brings *challenges*, and challenges create the *opportunity* to trust in God. Hallelujah!

Father, right now fill every one of our mothers with supernatural strength and healing. Renew their minds. Remove depression, anxious thoughts, and past hurts, in Jesus' name. Cover them with the precious and holy blood of Jesus Christ. Lord, bless and protect them. When they feel weak, remind them that is when you are strong. That the joy of the Lord is their strength.

We will never walk alone because you are with us, Lord God. You are with us, and we are all your children. Hallelujah! Thank you, Abba, for who you are. We love you, and give you all the glory. Have your way, Lord, have your way. In Jesus' name we pray. Amen.

# Day 38
## THANK HIM FOR HIS PROTECTION

Heavenly Father, thank you for waking us up on this awesome morning. You are so gracious, for you are not yet finished with us. We thank you; we glorify, honor, and give you all the glory and praise…because you deserve it all. Thank you, Lord, that we are your sons and daughters, seeking your presence before we start our day. We invite you in and ask that you have your way, in the precious wonderful name of Jesus. This is the day that the Lord has made, and we will rejoice and be glad in it!

Thank you for allowing us to see another blessed day and a glorious week. As we bow before the King, we come to thank you for everything. Thank you for the air we breathe, for our daily bread, and for allowing us to have a roof over our heads. We give you praise, Father God! Father, please supply and provide for those who are in pain, lonely, depressed, hungry, ill, or in need. Lord, we know that the enemy is relentless, so we pray for continued coverage under the blood of Jesus.

> *"Call to me and I will answer you and tell you*
> *great and unsearchable things you do not know."*
> ***(Jeremiah 33:3 NIV)***

Lord God, we thank you for using your power to accomplish your purposes through us, giving us the power to be all you want us to be, not who we want to be. Thank you for your ultimate plan. Help us to remember that we need to call on you. We must ask for your assistance because you can take care of our needs and the needs of others as we are standing in the gap like you chose us to do, in Jesus' name. The fervent prayer of the righteous availeth much. Hallelujah! Thank you that when are asking you, we are acknowledging that you alone are God and that we cannot accomplish anything in our own strength.

Father God, whenever we come before you, we are humbling ourselves, laying aside our willfulness and worry and determining to obey and trust in you. You are the King of Kings and the Lord of Lords. Thank you for drawing near to us. We appreciate you and are so grateful and thankful to be here, basking in your presence, coming into agreement, and standing in the gap for others, knowing that it is not about us but about *you*.

Lord, we pray that today, this week, and always that you place your angels around us and our loved ones to keep the enemy at bay, in Jesus' mighty name. Keep us covered under the precious blood of Jesus. We ask that you fill us with your supernatural strength to see us through. We lift up those who have to travel; we pray for traveling mercies and ask that you keep them in your arms. We pray for miraculous healing in this day for those who are not doing well in their body, mind, or soul. We speak for strength, peace, joy, and movement to come back into their lives, in Jesus' mighty name. We command every part that is not of you to leave. We cast it into the sea. We overturn every sickness by the blood of Jesus.

> *"'No weapon forged against you will prevail, and you will refute every tongue that accuses you. This is the heritage of the servants of the Lord, and this is their vindication from me,' declares the Lord."*
> **(Isaiah 54:17 NIV)**

We thank you, Lord, for your Word; your promises that you speak through us. Thank you for being with us in this very moment as you are in the midst of us. Thank you for each day that you have been with us, for your protection and provision for every need, as well as your grace that will sustain us. Help us, Lord God, to be a blessing to everyone around us, and may we bring you glory and honor in all that we say. Thank you for going before us and for drawing us closer in these troubled times.

> *"For the Spirit God gave us does not make us timid,*
> *but gives us power, love and self-discipline."*
> **(2 Timothy 1:7 NIV)**

Thank you, Jesus. I pray that your presence surrounds us, for we know that prayer changes everything. Thank you for your love and protection today and always.

Thank you, Lord, for who you are. We ask that you have your way in our lives because we cannot do anything on our own without you. Thank you for your timing because it is always perfect. You are so amazing, Abba. Thank you for your goodness in such a time as this. I pray that we will maintain our belief in an environment of unbelief and that we will continue to have faith in our everyday life…not just on the rainy days…because there are promises on the inside of us that our Almighty Lord God filled us with, in Jesus' name. Hallelujah! We know that where there are miracles happening, healings are coming.

> *"Now faith is confidence in what we hope for*
> *and assurance about what we do not see."*
> **(Hebrews 11:1 NIV)**

> *"Be still and know that I am God."*
> **(Psalm 46:10 NIV)**

Thank you that you are the Lord Almighty…you are who you say you are, and your promises are *"Yes"* and *"Amen."* When we can't see yet those promises materializing, we demonstrate true faith and trust in you, Lord. Thank you for who you are.

Father God, I declare that we will trust, dwell, enjoy safe pastures, delight, commit, rest, be still, and wait patiently for you, believing, trusting, and keeping our faith in you and your timing. We will submit to God and resist the devil because he will flee from us, in Jesus' name. We thank you for working out everything and causing your light to shine on us. We love you and praise you and pray all in Jesus' name. Amen.

# Day 39
## THANK HIM FOR FAMILY

Heavenly Father, what a gracious Father you are! We awoke this morning to experience another day. Thank you for everything you have bestowed on us. Thank you for the loyal and trustworthy friends and family that we have. There is no one else to thank but you because only you can do all good to us. Lord, as we come before you, we thank you for all the blessings in such a time as this. You are a good Father, and we give you the glory, honor, and praise because you deserve it all. We thank you for your Son Jesus who died for our sins. We love and appreciate you, and we are so grateful for you. Thank you for paying attention to us as we call on you.

> *"I will extol the Lord at all times; His praise will always be on my lips. My soul will boast in the Lord; let the afflicted hear and rejoice. Glorify the Lord with me; let us exalt His name together."*
> **(Psalm 34:1-3 NIV)**

Lord, thank you for the promises to your sons and daughters. It is joyful to know that we are yours. You are our Father, our Daddy God. Abba, have your way and do what you want to do in us and through us. Thank you that all things work together for the good of those who love you.

Father God, remind us that when we come before you, you are the one helping us to pray. We never need to be afraid of basking in your presence. Holy Spirit, please intercede for us, as we are in accordance with God's will. Father God, we know that you will always do what is best, so we thank you and give you the glory.

> *"The righteous cry out and the Lord hears them;*
> *He delivers them from all their troubles. The Lord is close to the*
> *brokenhearted and save those who are crushed in spirit."*
> **(Psalm 34:17-18 NIV)**

We know that you are able to do exceedingly abundant and amazing things. We trust in you and walk by faith, not by sight. Father God, we ask that you pour out your love all over us right now. Breathe on us. We need a touch from you—a breath from Heaven. We know that your Spirit is powerful and gives us life and fresh air; a fresh feeling when our hearts are heavy. Lord, we love others; not just our family, but those that you have placed in our path. We know at times that all is not well; and that is why we stand in the gap, coming into agreement, and believing for miraculous healing, joy, and love. We ask for things to be removed from the lives of those who struggle with addiction, depression, anxiety, strongholds, suicidal thoughts, bitterness, and anger.

Lord, we know that only you can set them free. Heal them, deliver them, and touch them with a mighty powerful touch, in Jesus' name. Lord, the value of a person is inside, and we know you know it all. We know that no person is too disgusting for you to touch. So Lord, we ask you right now for your mighty touch to come upon your people, in Jesus' name. Let your will be done on earth as it is in Heaven. We need a change from you because we know that it can and will change everything. One touch from you changes *everything*.

> *"Jesus was filled with compassion. He reached out his hand and*
> *touched the man. 'I am willing,' he said. 'Be clean!'"*
> **(Mark 1:41-42 NIV)**

Thank you for sending your Son and giving us the opportunity to be healed. Jesus, we ask that you send your great cure…your great miracle to the nation, to every community in this world just like you did with the incurable leprosy. We know that only you can cure all, and we call on your name, your touch, and your compassion. Please reach out to those who are not doing well and may be sick with pain and suffering. Heal them from head to toe with your touch, if you are willing. Lord, we know your Word says you are willing. Let your will be done.

We thank you in advance for working, Lord. We give you glory and honor. We thank you for being close to the brokenhearted. You are our source of power, courage, and wisdom, helping us through every problem, difficulty, frustration, sorrow, grief, loss, and failure. God, thank you that when these times come, we can admit that we need you because your help is amazing. You give us strength, peace, love, and joy, and we thank you for being by our side.

Remind us, Father God, that our ability and strength comes from the One who can do all things.

> *"But He said to me, 'My grace is sufficient for you, for My power is made perfect in weakness.' Therefore, I will boast all the more gladly about my weaknesses, so that Christ's power may rest on me."*
> **(2 Corinthians 12:9 NIV)**

Thank you for your power and strength. I pray that we will rely on you rather than our own energy, effort, or talent. Weakness not only helps develop Christian character—but it also deepens our worship because in admitting our weakness, we affirm God's strength. Hallelujah!

Thank you, Lord. We love and honor you. Have your way in Jesus' name. Amen.

# Day 40
## PRAISE HIM IN THE MOMENT

Almighty Father God, we thank you for who you are. God, you are gracious. You are our strength.

*"The Lord is my light and my salvation—whom shall I fear? The Lord is the stronghold of my life—of whom shall I be afraid?"*
**(Psalm 27:1 NIV)**

Daddy God, we thank you for waking us up this morning. Our first blessing in our life is that we are alive…and that is a whole lot we should be thankful for. We made it to another day. Thank you, Jesus. I pray that we do something today to take care of ourselves and that we find something positive in our life to make us feel better…because Lord, you wanted us to know this morning that we deserve to feel better and to do something good for ourselves, in Jesus' name. We may not have the money but remind us that it is not about the money, it is about taking care of ourselves.

If you haven't been out the house this week, go for a walk around the block. Listen to your favorite song or find something that touches you and puts joy in your heart because He has been good to you. You deserve a moment to treat yourself and feel better today. You are God's sons and daughters. Let today be a day that something will help improve your mood and attitude, and help give you relief from worry, anxiety, frustrations, and a heavy heart.

> ## GOD LOVES US, AND THERE IS NOTHING WE CAN DO ABOUT IT. WE CAN TRY BUT IT'S NOT GOING TO WORK.

Thank you for loving us the way you do. We praise you. We glorify you. All glory goes to you. We are more than conquerors.

> *"No, in all these things we are more than conquerors through him who loved us. For I am sure that neither death nor life, nor angels nor rulers, nor things present nor things to come, nor powers, nor height nor depth, nor anything else in all creation, will be able to separate us from the love of God in Christ Jesus our Lord."*
> **(Romans 8:37-39 NIV)**

Hallelujah!

Thank you, God, for your promises. We are not abandoned by Christ even when we have to face hardships in many forms: persecution, illness, imprisonment, and even death. As believers, I pray that we remember that it is impossible to be separated from Christ. Jesus' death is proof of His unstoppable love. Hallelujah! Nothing can stop Christ's constant presence with us.

Thank you for your love that makes us feel totally secure in you, Lord God. I come against the lies and works of the enemy, in Jesus' name. In Christ we are super conquerors (overcomers), and His love will protect us from any such forces.

> *"The Lord is my strength and my shield; my heart trusts in Him, and I am helped. My heart leaps for joy and I will give thanks to Him in song. The Lord is the strength of His people, a fortress of salvation for His anointed one. Save Your people and bless Your inheritance; be their shepherd and carry them forever."*
> **(Psalm 28:7-9 NIV)**

Thank you, Lord God, for your promises. You are so worthy and faithful. I declare that we will put our trust in you so that we may be helped through you. Thank you, Lord, for being enthroned a King forever. The King of Kings and the Lord of Lords. Your great power is so amazing. We can trust you to give us the peace and strength to weather the storms of life. Thank you for revealing your power through mighty miracles in our lives. Thank you that the power that controls creation and raises the dead is available to us, in Jesus' name. Hallelujah. We praise you, Daddy God. You deserve it all, for without you we can do nothing. I declare we will depend and rely on you, in Jesus' name.

I pray that today will be filled with the peace that passeth all understanding and guards our hearts and minds. God loves and cares for us. I pray that we will give everything to Him and face our day with confidence. Trust God. He's got our backs. I declare that we will have no complaints, no worries, no struggles, no anxious thoughts…that we will cast them into the sea and command them to leave, in Jesus' mighty name. Have your way, Lord. Thank you for who you are. We love you and appreciate you. We magnify and lift you up. We pray all in Jesus' mighty name. Amen.

# RESOURCES

Are you in need of prayer? We have a Prayer Line that is open and waiting for the privilege of praying with you and for you. Sponsored by Pastor Joey and Sunshine Miranda and hosted by JoAnn Latasha Smith-Figures, you can call Monday through Friday at 8:00 am.

*NGC Prayer Line: (612)746-7364 Code: 256707*

# ABOUT THE AUTHOR

JoAnn LaTasha Smith-Figures, a native of Chicago, IL, has been a Born-again Christian since 2012 and has been baptized in the name of Jesus. She holds an associate degree in General Studies from Coffeyville Community College and a bachelor's degree in Sports Management from Stetson University, and has been walking in Christ since 2012. She was delivered from a lifestyle of homosexuality and overcame a learning disability through the power of prayer, the blood of Jesus and the Holy Spirit's guidance. JoAnn is a walking, talking miracle, having survived a horrific car accident which almost killed her in 2019. After all that she has gone through, she testifies that she is a New Creation in Christ Jesus.

JoAnn is a member of Northgate Church in Hammond, Indiana, where she is involved in the Intercessory Prayer Group and has been given the opportunity to host the Prayer Line each weekday morning at 8:00 am.

## CONTACT THE AUTHOR

If you would like to contact the author, you may do so at smithjoann344@yahoo.com.

**Website**: http://jlsunwaveringfaith.com/

www.ingramcontent.com/pod-product-compliance
Lightning Source LLC
Chambersburg PA
CBHW072004290426
44109CB00018B/2131